It's Time!

D1649296

For Household Salvation The Unclaimed Promise of God

By Philip Cameron

Mainroads Productions Inc.
310 Judson Street, Unit 14
Toronto, Ontario
M8Z 1V3

1st printing – 10,000 – December 1986
2nd printing – 20,000 – February 1987

Copyright 1986 © MAINROADS PRODUCTIONS INC.

ISBN 0-919463-14-2

Published by MAINROADS PRODUCTIONS INC.
310 Judson Street, Unit 14, Toronto, Ontario M8Z 1V3

Printed in Canada
Harmony Printing Limited
123 Eastside Drive, Toronto, Ontario M8Z 5S5

The Publisher and Philip Cameron wish to thank Brian Paterson
and Paul Knowles for their invaluable assistance in the writing and
editing of this book.

The author would like to dedicate this book
to his mother and father
Simon and Wendy Cameron

CONTENTS

FOREWORD

I first saw Philip Cameron in the late sixties. He was a teenager with a difference. He wore a kilt, as did his preacher dad, his mom, his sisters, as well as his adopted brother and a cousin. In a day when families are torn apart by circumstances or, I hate to admit it, by choice, the Camerons, singing the songs their family wrote and made famous around the world such as, "All over the world, the Spirit is moving", "The Holy Ghost will set your feet a dancing", "Making melody in your heart" and others, sounded a clear message that God makes the difference!

When Philip arrived in Toronto in January, 1986, little did I know what God had in mind to do through this young preacher. On 100 Huntley Street, Canada's daily Christian television ministry, he exhorted us to believe God for the eternal salvation of our loved-ones. God spoke to us through him, and within a month we had put together a two week on air campaign to challenge the nation's believers to pray their loved-ones in. Almost 1,000,000 names were either telephoned or written in. Mighty reports of answered prayer began to come in, and they're still coming in. We then booked Philip on a nation wide tour of 50 cities for Household Salvation Rallies, and hundreds of family members gave their lives to Christ.

There is no doubt God has used this young Scot to spark a mighty outpouring of His Spirit in our Land. Those "Household Salvation" names were taken to the World Exposition, Expo '86 in Vancouver, British Columbia, Canada, where they remained for 5½ months under the altar in the chapel at the Pavilion of Promise, an evangelistic outreach we sponsored to the millions of visitors from around the world. I'll never forget the day when I saw a lady weeping near the altar. She was looking at the man and three young people who sat on the front pew. They had just made first time decisions for Jesus and were filling in their commitment cards. Not wanting to disturb the atmosphere, I communicated with her in signs. I pointed to the names behind the glass case on the altar and back at her husband, she said "yes" again. There they were, giving their lives to Christ, just five feet from where their names had been lovingly placed without their knowledge.

I could tell you hundreds of stories about Household Salvation, but this is not my book. I have now taken those precious names to the Cameron's Bible College in Peterhead, Scotland, where they have been lovingly placed in the prayer chapel. May I say for all, "Thank you Philip Cameron".

What can I say about one of the mightiest conversion stories ever, that of Philip's dad, Simon? You'll read it in the book, and your life will never be the same.

David Mainse
Host of "100 Huntley Street",
Toronto, Canada

INTRODUCTION

We live in perilous times. On one hand, prosperity — on the other, a seemingly unstoppable wave of sin. It often seems that the church has lost touch with the pertinent realities of life, while nations and continents slide toward doom. So many people are caught up with the cosmetics of Christianity, rather than facing and correcting the terrible problems that, if left unsolved, will destroy not only the Church, but the world.

Christians are the earth's salt, the essence of real life in an unreal world. We are God's examples — epistles known and read by those with whom we share our lives.

But somewhere, we have failed in that responsibility. I am disturbed — no, dismayed — by our apparent inability to maintain a generation to generation flow of the truth and promise of God. In this book I intend, with the help of God, to shed light and give hope to the mother, father, spouse, child, and anyone else who yearns to see the lost members of his or her family come to Jesus.

In this generation, the family is under more pressure to break apart than at any other time in history. As people have to try harder to survive in the rat-race, more and more become unable to fully cope with the dual responsibilities of work and parenthood. Children who already live in a sin-wracked society are given more time and more money to themselves, and thus they become prime targets of Satanic attack. It is a fact that the decline of the family has played a significant part in the demise of every great civilization. We, in this generation, simply do not have time to waste, if we are to act to prevent Satan from claiming the eternal souls of our loved-ones.

I intend to show you that God is indeed able to act in your family's situation. As you read about the experience of the Cameron family, and then go on to discover the extent of the promises of Household Salvation in God's Word, I trust that you will be challenged to begin the process of winning your entire family to Jesus.

It is time to make a stand, to break from our death-dealing lethargy. I pray that this small contribution will help someone to rise up with the tide of God and say, "IT'S TIME TO CLAIM THE UNCLAIMED PROMISE — HOUSEHOLD SALVATION!!"

Chapter One

The Camerons

The part of the Cameron clan from which I come is typical of many families in Scotland and around the world. There was a total lack of knowledge of who Jesus is and what He could do, and therefore, the darkness of sin dominated every aspect of Cameron life. That "darkness" can take many forms — in our family, it was alcoholism. Generations of my family were bound in a vicious cycle of drunkenness, seemingly with no end in sight.

But God is a wonder-worker and is, as Scripture states, "not willing that any should perish" (II Peter 3:9). In our situation, we had no personal contact with the gospel, so God had to arrange a meeting. In His mercy, He made sure that His love would be shown to our sin-laden family.

I call them "anointed moments." They are marvellous encounters between God and man. We see such moments in Eden's Garden, when God communed with Adam and Eve, and at the temple, when Simeon and Anna beheld the Christ child. These special times when God reaches down to touch a human heart have always occurred, and, as long as this dispensation of Grace lasts, they always will. The heart of the Father continually longs for restoration of fellowship with fallen man. The "anointed moment" for your loved-ones is on its way. The Great Arranger is at work, and your prayer and active faith will hasten that glorious day!

The Town Drunk

My Father, Simon Peter Cameron, is the youngest of seven children born to Michael and Christina Cameron. Christina came from the extreme north-west of Scotland and spoke Gaelic, the original language of my homeland. Like many other highland girls, she followed the fishing fleet from port to port. These were strong young women who made their livelihood packing the fish into barrels and boxes.

She met my Grandfather while working in the fish industry in Peterhead. By that time, Grandfather had already inherited the curse of the Camerons — he was an alcoholic. When he was barely seventeen, he had lied about his age to join the army during the first world war. In many horrible battles, he saw the lives of most of his friends snuffed out, one by one, as they clambered out of the muddy trenches into a hail of bullets. Only a handful of young men returned to our part of Scotland.

Rum and whiskey were given to the troops in order to instill false courage, and Michael always got his share. Eventually, he was sent home with shrapnel wounds in the head and back, suffering with dysentry, and trapped by an even more dangerous affliction — he was bound by alcohol.

He promised Christina that his drinking was a thing of the past, but that pledge of sobriety was forgotten almost as soon as they were married, and a pattern was established that lasted for over forty years. Many times, while on a drunken spree, my Grandfather would end up completely paralysed by liquor, and he would disappear for up to six weeks at a time. Sometimes they would find him lying in the street with his arms wrapped around his two dogs, Fanny and Flossy. Only their body heat kept him from freezing to death.

My father remembers one occasion when Granddad had sneaked out of his bedroom window with his new suit — a rare luxury — under his arm. He planned to sell it for enough money to buy more drink. But on that occasion, my Grandmother intercepted him. Her stubborn will, forged in the fires of necessity, prevailed, and the suit was hung back in the closet.

Raising seven children whose ages spanned less than twelve years, in the nineteen-twenties and thirties, was difficult at best, but when the problem of drunkenness was added, the situation became nearly impossible. There was little enough money anyway, and every shilling spent on drink added to the difficulties.

My Grandmother found unusual ways of augmenting the family income. They lived within a stone's throw of the North Sea, and when the fishing boats landed their catch at the pier, Grandmother would be waiting. When fish fell out of the boxes, as they were transported from ship to shore, she would gather them up. After accumulating a basketful, she walked many miles into the countryside, visiting the farms that surrounded the town. At farm after farm, she would knock on the doors and offer the fish for sale or barter. Only great need forced this shy girl from the Hebrides to do this, but she was determined to keep her family together and to meet their needs.

She was barely able to do so, and in those desperate days, there was little or no hope of ever improving what seemed to be an unchangeable situation.

An "Anointed Moment"

War swept over all of Europe in 1939, even reaching to the ports of northern Scotland. The eldest son of Michael and Christina Cameron, Michael Jr., went to work for the British Iron and Steel Corporation. The United States had not yet entered the war, but was supplying lease-lend materials to Great Britain to help in the war effort. Their ships became targets for Nazi air and submarine attack. When the ships were hit, the brave men would try to salvage the cargo and even the metal of the ship itself.

A ship had been beached on the Island of Stroma, one of the small islands off the coast of Scotland. Young Michael was part of the crew assigned to salvage the vessel. Stroma lies just over a mile from the mainland, and although it is deserted today, it was once a thriving community of many families. Michael lodged at one of the farms on the island.

Although he was only in his late teens, Michael had already followed in his father's footsteps — he was under the bondage of alcohol, and was well-known on the island for his drinking habits. While he was stationed on Stroma, he would take advantage of any leave to go over to the mainland for liquor. The only means of transportation available was a small boat owned by an old man with one leg, who would row passengers over and back for a shilling. Michael would get drunk and then return to Stroma with as many bottles of alcohol as he could carry.

On one such trip to the mainland, Michael left the boat intending to purchase a supply of liquor, but ended up with much more than he had planned for. Something happened which was to change the entire path of the Cameron family.

He walked to a small cafe for a cup of tea. As he waited for the waitress to bring his order, his glance fell on a small piece of paper wedged between the salt and pepper shakers. Reaching over, he picked it up and began to read.

He read about the Creator, and about man, sin and bondage. He felt like the author had been writing about Michael, himself. He read on, to learn about Jesus coming to earth, about the manger and about the love shown at Calvary, and the grace of God demonstrated. Then the "anointed moment" came. Suddenly the revelation of grace dawned on his sin-sick heart. He was keenly aware of his sin and his shame, and in total simplicity, he rolled his burden on Jesus.

God had broken through! A beachhead had been established in the Cameron family. The young man who had left Stroma Island a sinner had come face to face with the love of God, and had passed from death unto life, through grace.

He returned to Stroma and began to tell everyone on the island about what God had done. His mind turned to Peterhead and home — his family had to know! Jesus would do the same for them! Michael, in his new-found faith, did not realise what was ahead for him — seven years in which he would stand alone against the ridicule of his own family.

As he climbed those familiar steps to the kitchen of the Cameron home in Peterhead, his heart was racing with joy. He was ready to share his story — he couldn't wait to see the reaction of those he loved. He dropped his small suitcase at his feet, and stood with his raincoat folded over his arm. He began to talk, speaking to everyone at once, telling of the great things that had taken place in his heart. He told the family of the cafe, the gospel tract, the grace, the forgiveness, the joy, and the peace. It poured from him in an emotional torrent.

And then he told them that the good news was for them, too! Things didn't have to be the way they had been for so long — there was a better way! God could deliver them, and set them free!

Instead of a joyful reception, Michael was faced with a stoney silence. Each member of the family was baffled by this strange thing that had happened to Michael. The Bible says: "The god of this world hath blinded the minds of them which believe not" (II Corinthians 4:4), and that was certainly true of the Cameron family. Instead of seeing the wonder of what had happened to Michael, they wondered what was wrong with him!

You would think that someone who was in bondage would grasp at any opportunity to be free. No matter how stupid the idea might seem to be, it would be worth a try. People, however, do not always think that way.

Michael Jr. had left Stroma Island, and was working at home again. Each day at lunch time, he would come home, quickly gulp down his lunch, and then go into his bedroom to pray. Michael had received a promise from the Lord: "If you remain faithful, I will save your whole family". Michael was convinced that the power of sin would be broken and that God would fulfill His promise of HOUSEHOLD SALVATION.

In those days, long before television, the Camerons entertained themselves by sitting

16

around the fire and singing songs or telling stories to pass a long winter's night. On one of those occasions, Michael was asked to sing in his strong, sweet voice. The family expected to hear one of his many secular songs, but instead, he began to sing, "On a hill far away stood an old rugged cross, the emblem of suffering and shame . . .". When he came to the verse, "To that old rugged cross I will ever be true, its shame and reproach gladly bear," Michael broke down, and left, weeping, to return to his bedroom.

The rest of the family, feeling extremely uncomfortable, decided that this simply had to stop. Michael was going insane! They had to try to snap him out of whatever this "thing" was that he had fallen into. Their efforts failed. For seven long, lonely years young Michael prayed, holding to God for the fulfillment of the promise: "Remain faithful and I will save your whole family".

During those years my Grandfather continued to drink, and eventually his business began to deteriorate. Things got so bad that he made a promise to God: "Save my business and I will serve You". The financial crisis passed — but so did the promise, and Granddad continued in the same old way.

Chapter Two

Love at First Sight

Michael Jr.'s youngest brother, Simon Peter — my father — was a teenager, and just about to leave school, where he was known as "Professor", because he was always the top of his class. He was frequently urged to continue on to university, but with the self-destructive hoplelessness that was typical of the Camerons in those days, he declined. He knew there was no money, and therefore no point in trying to continue. Instead, he went to work with his Dad and his brothers in the junk metal business.

In spite of his good marks in school, he had a very low sense of self-worth: he was the youngest of seven children, always wore other people's cast-offs, and, worst of all, was the son of the town drunk.

One night, Dad joined his brothers Alex and John at a dance. I know this sounds like a movie script, but he saw her across the dance floor. Her name was Wendy. She was a red-head, and was laughing and enjoying herself as she danced in someone else's arms. Eventually Dad plucked up enough courage to ask her to dance. By the end of the evening, the sixteen-year old lad was head over heels in love with that vivacious red-head.

Wendy was eighteen, and a pharmacist's apprentice. She and her sister, Christian, had lived with their uncle Lionel and their Grandmother, since their parents divorced when Wendy was six. In his mid-thirties, Lionel married, and his new wife, Yolande, became a close friend to her new niece.

To Dad's surprise, Wendy was willing to continue to see him; to his utter amazement, she returned his love. For the first time in his life, he was at the centre of someone's attention, instead of being at the end of a line of seven.

As they walked hand-in-hand one night, Wendy asked, "How old are you?"

"Guess," challenged Dad.

"Nineteen."

Dad smiled. "Close," he said, enjoying the fact that she took him at his word. Even today we tease our mother that, if Dad said the moon was made of green cheese, she'd believe it.

His age was not his only embarrassment in the growing relationship. Eventually Mum asked him, "What kind of business is your family in?"

Ashamed to admit that they bought and sold junk metal and old clothes (in Scotland the term is "rag and bone merchant"), Dad replied, "Do you know what a spirit-level is?"

Wendy nodded.

"Well, we make the little bubbles that float in the fluid to tell whether a wall is level." Again, she believed him.

(Let me note that while Dad could always pull this off, I have never had that effect on my Mother. From birth to now, she has been able to see straight through me, sometimes sensing my moods and needs all the way across the Atlantic Ocean).

Wendy continued to love dancing. Although her new aunt, Yolande, did not go to dances or even approve of them, she would iron Wendy's dress and clean her shoes. This allowed the young girl to rush through supper and leave immediately for the dance.

One night, as she dressed, Wendy asked, "Yolande, why is it that even though you disapprove of dancing, you help me to get ready each time?"

Even as a smile crossed Yolande's face, Wendy could see a certain sadness in her aunt's eyes. "Wendy, you're right. I don't approve of worldly things," she said. The first spiritual seed in Wendy's life was about to be sown. She continued, "This is your heaven. It's the only heaven you will ever know. If this is all there is going to be for you, I want you to enjoy it."

Wendy's heart sank. She went to the dance that night, but as she swept across the floor, her mind was far from the evening's entertainment.

"Is this all there is?" she asked herself. "Surely there is more to life than this."

God had begun a work — Wendy's "anointed moment" was on the way!

Crisis!

Dad and Mum's love for each other grew and deepened, and in spite of family opposition they began to plan and dream together. She would be a pharmacist; he somehow would make good, although to anyone looking on, his task was formidable at best. And just when things seemed to be getting better, the bottom fell out of their world.

Dad stood shivering in the cold winter night, his eyes fixed on a window of the house across the street. The cold was forgotten, for he was much more concerned with what was happening inside that house.

Finally the door opened, and Wendy emerged, slowly slipping her purse over her shoulder, and walking, with head bowed, toward her sixteen-year-old boyfriend. The moment that their eyes finally met, he knew without words that their world, already bleak, was now destroyed. Wendy was going to have a baby.

She was brave in the face of the disaster, and as he walked her home she offered to go it alone. He was too young to be married, and if he wanted to be free, that was all right with her.

Simon was determined to marry his Wendy, but his parents were completely opposed to the marriage. He told them of their plight that night, and his mother put her foot down, hard — he was too young, needed their approval, and wasn't going to get it!

From the flurry of emotions that beseiged the overpowered young man, one thought emerged: "If I can't have Wendy as my wife, I'd be better off dead."

He knew where to find the full bottle of tablets, and he dumped the entire contents into his hand. Sipping water between every few tablets, he had soon gulped them all.

His first thought was, "I've got to see Wendy one more time." He ran out of the front door, and all the way to her home. Her guardians still knew nothing of what happened — she had been afraid to tell them, because they had never had much time for this boy from the wrong side of the tracks.

Glancing from the window, Wendy saw her young, frightened boyfriend beckoning her outside. But as they spoke, he did not tell her what he had done. They talked softly and held each other close. As Dad began to feel the effect of the tablets, he quickly said goodbye. He watched longingly as she turned and went into her house — he had lost everything. There was no hope.

He turned homeward, wanting only to climb into his bed, and to die.

How he managed to make it all the way home is still a mystery. He was dizzy, and very ill. He lunged through the door, raced into the bathroom and was violently sick. As he vomited, he thought, "I'll just have to die here."

The next thing he knew, his mother was kneeling beside him. In his haste he had forgotten to lock the bathroom door, and she had rushed in after him. She realized what her broken-hearted son had done, and she began to weep.

Dad had never seen his mother cry. All those years of having to be mother, father and provider for her seven children had hardened her. But kneeling on the bathroom floor, she was broken, to my father's astonishment. She said, "I love you, Simon. I don't want to lose you. If Wendy means this much to you, then I will give you permission to get married."

The vomiting had saved his life, so that immediate danger was over.

After speedy arrangements between the two families, the time for the wedding was at hand. Simon and Wendy were to be married on January 24, 1948.

Dad sat shivering and nervous in the car which was heading for the small Registrar's office where the civil wedding ceremony was to be performed. Hectic days and weeks had passed since that terrifying night in which near-tragedy had turned into a parent's blessing.

The quickly planned wedding was an added

strain for the Cameron family, for Dad's older brother, John, was to be married soon after Dad and Mum's wedding.

John and his bride-to-be had received many more gifts than Simon and Wendy. Their hurried event gave little time for basic planning, let alone for wedding gifts. But one night, as the wedding dates drew near, some friends brought a gift of dishes to John. He wasn't there, so grandmother thanked the givers on behalf of her son — and then placed them carefully beside the few items that her youngest son, Simon, had received. Several more gifts were "liberated" in this way. Until now, no one has known of this except my Father.

In the car with Dad, on the way to the Registrar's, was his eldest sister, Chrissie. She fussed over her young brother's clothes, smoothed his hair, and gave a multitude of last minute instructions, all of which fell on deaf ears! Dad was thinking only of his Wendy. But suddenly he heard Chrissie ask a question he hadn't heard before: "Do you have enough money for the marriage license?"

His blank stare changed in an instant to one of panic! "Oh, no!" cried the startled bridegegroom. "I don't have any money!"

Chrissie shook her head, imagining the disasters that this day seemed bound to produce. But then she rummaged through her purse until she found the necessary one pound note, which she thrust unto her brother's hand.

A relationship that began as a night at a dance had resulted in a hastily arranged marriage. The young couple had no money, no home — and no future. Another generation of Camerons began with all the dice loaded against them.

The one thing Dad and Mum did have was

love. Even living in his parent's crowded home did not diminish the enjoyment they derived from one another's company. And the ability to laugh was always part of their love.

Each day brought them closer to the birth of their baby. At night, as they lay in the darkness, they would talk about the future, and make great plans. They promised each other that "This baby will have a better chance than we did." They determined to give this new Cameron all the things that the Camerons had not known.

"What will we call our wee one?" Mum would ask.

Dad would always respond, "If it's a boy, we'll call him Simon Alan." They were sure it would be a boy.

One day, Mum greeted Dad with a secretive smile, and said, "Simon, why don't you come up to Uncle Lionel's tonight after work? I have a surprise for you." Dad knew Mum well enough that he didn't question her, he simply showed up — and "surprise" was not adequate to describe his reaction.

"Follow me," beamed Wendy, and she led him through her Aunt and Uncle's house, out the back door and into the garden, to a small wooden garden shed. That shed, which measured six by twelve feet, was now furnished as a tiny home. Mum had hunted for the furniture, and had somehow found a couch-bed, a small table with two chairs, a skinny wardrobe and a throw-rug. There was a tiny wood stove in one corner. With the magic touch of love, she had somehow turned a garden shed into a home. The young couple ran an extension cord to the shed, and hung one single light in the room.

On the door Wendy had written, in yellow paint, "Simon and Wendy's hut." They moved in that night.

Excitement grew right along with Mum's tummy. But though she was bigger every day, Mum's pace did not lag. She was healthy, and eager for the birth of her first-born. The baby was to be born at Simon's parents' home, under the care of a wonderful and brilliant doctor, a man who was to play an important part in Simon and Wendy's life.

My father has always had a low pain threshold — for his own pain, and for anyone else's, as well. On one occasion, while we were vacationing in Wales, I fell and split my head open. The local doctor was summoned, and when he arrived at the camp-site at which we were staying, he realised that he had left his surgical needle and thread at home. He casually asked if there was a regular needle and thread available.

At this, Dad lunged toward the wardrobe — which happened to contain the sewing equipment — and began to rummage furiously. Soon a shoe flew back over his shoulder, followed immediately by its mate.

"Simon," said Mother, "I know exactly where it is. Let me look."

Father shot a frenzied glance back at his wife. "Wendy," he exclaimed, "I'm not looking for the needle. I want my coat!" With that, he was off. Despite the crisis at hand, everyone, even the doctor, could not hold back their laughter.

Dad had the same kind of struggles when it was time for the baby to be born. When Mum gave the first indication of labour, Dad began to panic. The rest of the family teased him that the doctor would have to treat him before caring for the mother and child!

When the pains were frequent enough that the doctor was called, Dad left before the doctor arrived. He ran out, "borrowed" a neighbour's bike, and made his escape. As he peddled away, he noticed that the wind, which usually blew in from the sea, was gusting strongly from inland, impeding his progress.

"Just my luck! Even the wind is against me," he thought, as he struggled to reach the crest of the hill. Little did he forsee the real storm that was looming on his horizon.

It was a breach birth. The good doctor worked very hard to make this first birth as easy as possible for the young girl he had known for years, and of whom he was very fond. And after a great struggle, Simon Alan Cameron was born, a seven pound boy. A tired, aching mother waited for her husband to return.

Simon entered the house, brave now that the struggle was over! "He's the most beautiful baby in the world," he declared. "Wendy, he looks just like me!"

Wendy smiled. Although little Simon Alan had been born in difficult circumstances, he would be loved. He would have a better life than they had known. The doctor ordered complete bed-rest until she recovered from the difficult birth, but although she was temporarily confined to bed, her mind was as active as ever, and her thoughts raced ahead to the happy days to come.

The baby was three days old, and Mum was beginning to feel much better. She was impatiently waiting for the first opportunity to go out and walk down the street in our town, to proudly show off her little bundle of joy. The baby was warm and soft in her arms, as she held the bottle gently in his tiny mouth.

But her day-dreaming stopped instantly as she looked down at her son. He had stopped sucking, and immediately, she knew something was wrong. Fighting back panic, she nudged the nipple up and down to get a response, but there was none.

"Simon," she screamed, "Something's wrong with the baby!" As she spoke, she tore open her nightdress and held the wee baby close to her warm body — the eighteen-year old girl wanted to give her warmth to her son, somehow thinking this would make him well.

"Get the doctor! My baby's not breathing right!"

The young father's heart felt as though it would burst as he once again struggled to peddle up that steep hill. The "borrowed" bike did not seem to respond to his furiously pumping legs. The doctor who had delivered the baby was not close at hand, and Dad rushed to the office of the nearest doctor, even though he was a stranger to the Cameron family. Impelled by panic and fear, he rushed straight through the waiting room, right into the doctor's office. Through his tears, Dad blurted, "Doctor, come quickly! My baby's dying!"

Enraged, the doctor ordered him out of the room. "I'm with a patient! You wait until I've finished. Anyway, If it's as bad as you say, the child is probably dead by now!"

Simon waited for what seemed to be an eternity in the corridor outside the office. Finally, from the doorway, he heard the doctor give some instructions to his patient about taking some cough medicine. He then turned to the weeping young man.

"Now, what's your problem?" asked the annoyed physician. "And besides, am I your doctor?"

"No", gasped Dad, "I came here because you were closest for my baby." Dad told him the name of their own family doctor.

The man turned back into his office. "I can't come, but I will call your own doctor." Before he dialed the phone, he snapped at Dad, "Go home! He'll be there as soon as he can."

Dad left the office. He turned the bicycle homeward, terrified of what would be waiting for him.

When Dad reached the top of the hill, he saw the doctor's black car parked haphazardly in the street outside the house. The presence of the medical man sparked hope in the heart of the newly-turned-seventeen-year old father.

But his hope was empty. Mum had been rocking the limp baby in her arms. A tiny trickle of water ran from the infant's nose. Through her tears, she called out to God, "Please don't take my baby!". But in spite of the diligent efforts of the doctor, he could not save the child. He was dead. Three days of joy had turned into a nightmare beyond anything the young couple could have imagined.

The storm had come. Wendy longed for the impossible — to see her baby again. Simon began to harden, as bitterness filled the void that Simon Alan had left.

The tiny white coffin was laid on the table covered with white cloth. The young couple sat, numb, as the preacher led the funeral service. Mum felt as if the book of her life had been slammed shut. And at that moment, Dad's brother and his wife brought their week-old baby in to visit. This was almost too much.

At the end of the service, they got in the taxi for the ride to the grave. The undertaker laid the small coffin on Dad's knee as they drove to the cemetery.

In one short year, Dad had learned to love, had almost died at his own hand, had married, had seen the birth of his own baby, and then — this. He could hardly bring himself to leave the open grave.

It is said that time heals all wounds, and to a certain measure, that is right. Slowly, things began to return to normal. But there were nights when Mum would awaken, screaming, as she dreamed of the baby lying limp in her arms. Or as she watched her sister-in-law cradle her own little girl, the baby would become Simon Alan, in Mum's mind.

Her longing for her child remained for many years, but in the back of Mum's mind was a strange assurance: "My baby is in heaven."

And all this time, Dad's brother Michael was praying faithfully, every day, for Household Salvation to come to the Camerons.

Chapter Three

Married to a Stranger

World War II had recently ended, but already, trouble was brewing in Korea. The continuing tensions meant that National Service was still in force, and when Simon reached the age of eighteen, he was drafted.

For the young couple, this seemed disastrous. How could they live without each other for two years?

Dad endured boot camp at a place called Ellesmere. He and Wendy would write, sharing everything that was happening in their very separate lives, as the weeks and months dragged by.

Finally, Mum could stand the separation no longer. On impulse, she caught the train and left Peterhead to join her husband. There were no allowances for married couples at boot camp, so Mum found lodgings with a nearby family. She took a part-time job, but spent every available minute with Dad. There were strict rules prohibiting civilians from being on Army property, but where there's a will, there's a way! In the evening, under the cover of darkness, Dad would smuggle Mum into his barracks, where he shared a room with a corporal. He would cover the window with the thick, coarse blanket from his bed, and sit and watch while Wendy shone his boots, polished his brass, and cleaned his bedspace. This labour of love earned Private Cameron top marks for his appearance, and the advantage he had over his fellow soldiers was never discovered.

Their time together in Ellesmere was marvellous, but when boot camp ended, the time for separation came again. While the units all around him were sent to Korea, Dad's unit was posted to a multi-national force in Trieste, in Northern Italy.

That change in residence led to more serious internal change in Simon. Away from home for the first time, he began to drink, and the pattern of drunkenness which had plagued the Camerons began to emerge. Instead of avoiding the terrible bondage of alcohol, Dad fell completely into the trap. His language deteriorated, and was soon so vile that his blasphemous use of Jesus' name caused a Corporal to comment, "Cameron, I don't mind you cursing, but must you use the name of Jesus with every second breath?"

At home, Michael Jr. was still praying, eagerly awaiting the day when his family would be saved. Seven years had passed since that moment in the cafe, but the promise had been given and Michael was faithful. He often preached to a small congregation of about twelve people in a little church in Peterhead.

Michael's Reward

Two recent graduates from Bible school were about to hold their very first Gospel Campaign. They had picked Peterhead as their launching point, and the services were to be held in a small room, up some stairs and around the back of a house on Broad Street. While they were in Peterhead, their home was a small, antiquated van — sort of a primitive motor home, with the emphasis very much on "primitive".

These two young evangelists, Herbert Harrison and Donald Walker did not know what was about to happen. Michael Cameron did not realise what was about to happen, either. But God knew!

They had planned a brief crusade, but it lasted six weeks. There were ninety-six converts, and more than sixty of them were named Cameron! The young men didn't know what to think as, each night, convert after convert gave the same name: "Cameron".

The Camerons were coming to Jesus!

Unlike her husband, my mother had always attended church. Yet, in almost eighteen years of church services, she had never heard the gospel! While she believed in God — the God to whom she had prayed as her baby was dying — she had never known Him as her personal Saviour.

Chrissie, Simon's sister, needed help. Mum thought that a little religion would straighten her sister-in-law's life out. "Let's go and hear the preachers tonight, Chrissie," Mum suggested.

"Okay," Chrissie replied, "I've nothing else to do."

They climbed the stairs and sat down in the tiny room where so many of the Camerons had been getting saved.

Mum was immediately shocked! Donald Walker was singing, and worse, he was smiling! He looked happy! This could not be a proper church. Where was the organ? Where were the candles? Some people were even clapping their hands.

"Oh, no," thought Mum, "what have I got myself into?" She tried to act as if there was nothing wrong. "I'm here to get Chrissie some religion," Mum the church-goer told herself, not realising that she was just as lost, as doomed as the sister-in-law sitting beside her.

When Herbert Harrison stood up to preach, Mum's suspicions were even greater. "Oh, no," she thought, "This isn't a real minister. Where are his robes? Where is his clerical collar? Why is he preaching in a normal tone of voice? Why is he so young?" Her eyes fell on the bright, Paisley-print tie which Harrison wore, and she wondered what her vicar would say! If he could see her now!

Worse still, the preacher declared, "Praise the Lord!" In shock, and unable to believe her eyes or her ears, she was convinced that she had made a terrible mistake.

Harrison announced his text and began to speak. Mum heard little of what he said, until he declared, "Thou fool, this night thy soul shall be required of thee" (Luke 12:20). That statement was like an arrow that pierced her soul. "For what is a man profited, if he shall gain the whole world and lose his own soul?" (Matthew 16:26). Suddenly her "anointed moment" was coming to be.

Her attention was riveted on the young preacher. Her mouth was dry, and her heart pounded within her. She ceased to be aware of Chrissie seated beside her, or of anyone else nearby. The spotlight of God was shining on her. She felt uncomfortable and unclean. What did she have to do to get rid of her sin? Harrison's words were drifting in and out of her consciousness. One minute she heard his voice, the next, her own thoughts. She heard him for a moment: "Confess your sin, and God is faithful and just to forgive." The preacher was pulling in salvation's net.

"Confess?" Mum began to worry. "Confess? I'll never remember all the things I've done wrong."

Suddenly the self-righteous, religious girl began to sense her own need of help.

"I'll just tell him the big sins," Mum thought, as

she raised her hand in answer to the preacher's appeal. "When I remember the smaller ones, then I'll confess those to him as well."

Harrison asked those who had raised their hands to come to the front of the room. Mum stood, and as she did, she was categorizing her sins from "bad" to "not so bad", in preparation to confess! She had become so engrossed in her own "anointed moment" that she did not see Chrissie come forward as well.

The Camerons were coming to Jesus!

Mum began to confess her sins to the preacher, but he interrupted her: "No, no sister. You don't confess to me. Tell Jesus!" Mum took her eyes of the man and turned them toward Jesus. She began to ask Jesus Christ to make her clean, and, just as the preacher had said, she felt her burden of sin roll away — she was born again! A dance hall would no longer be her only heaven. And best of all, she knew that she would see her baby again. A hope that had been futile now became an eternal assurance.

A lifetime of dead, unreal religion hadn't done as much for Wendy as two hours of reality. Ornate buildings with stained glass windows had failed, but the Lord Jesus Christ had made all the difference. As Chrissie and Mum walked home that night, their hearts burned within them, in excitement and joy.

Mum arrived back at the little shack, took off her hat and coat, and lay down on the bed. She began to think of the great change that knowing Jesus would make, and she thought about Dad. Ever since they had met, they had done everything together.

Mum sat upright in bed, thinking "Simon will be so pleased. He's going to have a brand new wife!" She reached for the writing paper that was their only contact across the miles between Peterhead and Trieste. As pen touched paper, the joy of what had happened poured out.

"My darling Simon, I have great news . . . I've fallen in love with Jesus. I'm going to be a different person when you come home." Mum was so excited at the thought of her soldier husband knowing about Jesus. This was the hope they needed — the start of a new and better life.

She waited anxiously for his response. During those days, her spirit soared as she imagined the two of them praying together, serving God together, and watching as Jesus made something beautiful of their lives. The Bible became her constant companion, and every spare moment was spent in studying God's word and His promises.

"Stop Before You go Too Far"

The Italian stamp and the "Trieste" postmark told her that her wait was over. Her answer had come. Once again her mind raced to the future, excited at the prospect of good news from Dad. She raced through her uncle's house and into the garden shed that was now her home. She sat down, took a deep breath, and carefully opened the letter.

"Dear Wendy . . .". Her stomach tightened into a knot. This was not how Simon usually began his letters.

"I have just received your letter explaining what you have done. I will not allow my wife to get involved with all this religious nonsense." Mum could hardly believe her eyes!

"I am telling you now: stop before you go too far. I'll give you 'gloriously saved' when I come home!"

Her cheeks were flushed, and she found it hard to breathe. This wasn't her Simon! It didn't seem like him at all! And in a very real sense it wasn't. He had tasted the sins of the world, and it seemed that nothing could satiate his thirst. The last thing in the world that he wanted was a "saved" wife.

Her fingers trembled as she folded the letter and placed it back in the envelope. She felt torn, pulled in two directions, between her love for Jesus and her love for Simon.

"I'm saved," she thought. "The preacher said that I've been born again." She recalled Dad's words — "Stop before you go too far." Dad's presence was almost tangible in the small room.

"I've been born again," Mum declared, aloud. "You can't be unborn once you're born." Her determined voice reflected the momentous decision she was making. "I'm going on. I can't stop serving Jesus. I'm going to pray for Simon to be saved. No matter what, I'm going to be faithful."

As with her brother-in-law Michael before her, the young woman did not realise what lay ahead, but she was determined to live for God.

Dad was to be in Italy for eighteen more months. Suddenly, the hours that had dragged seemed to fly by. She studied and prayed as if her life depended on it. Dad's stance did not change, and Mum knew that confrontation was inevitable. As each day passed, both fear and excitement grew in her heart. She desperately wanted to see her Simon again, but she was terribly afraid of what would happen when he came home.

The day finally came when Dad was demobilised from the army, and the young soldier returned to Peterhead.

The immediate difficulties were enormous and daunting. The man who returned from Italy was nothing like the person who had left. Mum felt that she was married to a stranger. The young man whom she had married, with whom she had laughed and played, was gone. In his place returned a vile and unfeeling person, with whom she had nothing in common.

Setting aside his former gentleness, Dad was determined to show Mum that he was the boss. He intended to turn the threats of his letters into reality. Every day, Mum prayed, asking God to show her how to love him.

Dad was literally hell-bent on having his way. The first thing to go was her Bible — he destroyed it, and refused to allow her to have another. He also prevented her from attending church; for three and a half years, Mum seldom was allowed to attend a service. She did manage to find fellowship with other Christians, however. When shopping, she would meet with other sisters in the Lord, and over a cup of tea, they would pray together. In this way, Mum found an invaluable source of encouragement.

On many occasions, Dad would decide to go to the movies or to a dance. In Scotland, even today, Christians do not attend such activities. Mum would refuse to go, but Dad would physically force her to accompany him. In the theatre, if Mum would not look at the screen, he would beat her. The Scripture is true: "What communion hath light with darkness?" (II Corinthians 6:14).

When things would get very bad, many people, even including some of the Christian women with whom she met, would advise Mum to get out before something really serious happened. But Mum would reply, "You don't understand. Simon is my husband, and we are one flesh. I'm going to walk in heaven with him some day." She knew that Michael had received the answer to his prayers, and she simply believed that God would do the same for her.

But at home, things only became worse. Simon was becoming more and more belligerent every day.

In spite of all of the bad news, there were bright spots, such as the day when Mum felt something stir within her, and recognized that feeling. Her visit to the doctor confirmed what she already knew.

Several months later, a baby girl was born. They called her Wendy. My mother could not have known just how much this little bundle would mean to her in the days ahead. At times, she seemed to be the only point of happiness in a life that was becoming more and more miserable.

Their living conditions were still very poor. When Wendy was only a few months old, she woke in her tiny cot in the little wooden hut, and began to cry. In the half-darkness, Mum and Dad could see her bottle lying near her face, but when they switched on the light, they discovered a large rat on top of her. It had eaten through the nipple of her bottle, and the milk splashing on her face had caused the baby to waken.

Mum had noticed that Dad's drinking, and all that accompanied his sinful life, had robbed him of any desire for self-advancement. He didn't care to improve his lot in life, or that of his family. He was bound, and he was blind to any chance of a brighter future.

Before the birth of their first child, Mum had entertained many dreams. Everything was to be perfect — but those dreams vanished like smoke when Simon Alan died. Now, with Wendy, there was only one thing that counted to Mum: "My daughter will know and love Jesus."

Even before she was born, Mum had sung songs about Jesus to her, and had told the child in her womb about Jesus' love. Based in that love, a special closeness grew between mother and daughter. As the wee girl grew up, her mother told her stories of heaven. When Wendy was only three years old, she said to her Mum, "I want to ask Jesus into my heart".

That transaction was for real, and has lasted all her life. My sister Wendy has been one of the mainstays of our family in our quest to serve God.

Several months before that precious moment when Wendy prayed with Mum, Mum had once again sensed the beginning of life within her. Once again, she was right — I was on my way.

My father worked with his brothers in a business he and Mum had started days after Wendy's birth. They sold nets to farmers and gardeners to cover newly sown seed. Dad lived a Jeckyll and Hyde existence — during the day, he was the hard-working youngest brother and son of the family, but at night, and when alone, he was a degenerate husband and father. In those critical days, my mother clung to the hope that, somehow, God would make a way. But at the moment, there seemed to be no way.

Her pregnancy, as she carried me, was difficult. A series of set-backs had dogged those months — no heartbeat, no movement, wrong position — bringing fresh fears with every pronouncement. Like my brother before me, my birth was very difficult. But finally, after a 42-hour labour, and with the aid of a brilliant doctor, I was born — rather squashed, but alive.

My birth had no impact on my father's life. Nothing changed, as one day blurred into the next. The Cameron family knew only hopelessness and recurring crisis. Mother began to wonder if he would ever be saved. She had prayed for seven years, and the dreams of their youth had long since vanished.

She became desperate, and one day, while Dad was at work, she knelt before God in prayer: "Oh, God, I don't know if I even like him any more. Please give me grace to stay with him for one more month."

Her prayer seemed to have the effect of a gas pedal, speeding up the already degenerating situation — Dad got even worse. But she did not cease her prayers.

The little hut had a sink and a drain that took the water out, but no faucet. Water had to be carried in, and heated in a kettle. Often, in the early hours of the morning, when my Dad was not yet home, Mum would be washing my diapers and putting them through the old hand wringer that was attached to the sink. Weary and discouraged, she would stop on the middle of her task, put her head on the wringer, and weep, praying, "Jesus, wherever Simon is, keep him safe. Bring him home to me. Give me grace, please give me grace to live with him just one more month."

But Dad just kept getting worse, and mother wondered how she was going to remain strong in her faith, not realising that underneath and all around are the everlasting arms of Jesus.

Mother would often speak to little Wendy, and somehow she seemed to understand the hurt her mother was feeling. On long nights when Dad was out, Wendy would be my Mum's little friend and confidant. Many times, when my mother was on the verge of giving up, her little girl would come up to her and say, "Mummy, could you please tell me about heaven?"

Mum would lift Wendy up on her lap, look into her brown eyes, hold her close and say, "Oh, yes, I'll tell you about heaven." Then she would describe the golden streets and the gates of pearl. She talked of the beauty of Jesus, and of the end of tears and trials. The waves of glory would begin to flow in my mother's heart, and after she tucked the wee lassie into her bed at night, and kissed her on the cheek, she would go back to the washing, and with new strength she would say to herself, "Well, I'll try again. I'll pray some more."

Because of the drink, darkness and sin, the Simon that she now lived with was totally different from the Simon she had married. Once, he had been a soft-hearted, likeable young boy who respected her and treated her with a love that was sometimes close to worship. Now, he was a hardened drunk who abused and misused her.

Many times he would come in drunk at four o'clock in the morning. The amazing thing is that, in those early morning hours, when most wives would have told their husbands to get lost, my mother had dinner ready for him. Often he would be too drunk even to get ready for bed, but she would undress him and put him into bed. Sometimes she would quietly pray over him, but he was so full of hatred that he would curse at her, and blame her Jesus for the mess that their marriage was in.

Eventually, her secret prayer was not for enough strength to last a month, but enough to last seven days: "God, help me to live with him for one more week." The more she prayed, the worse he got. She didn't realise it, but God was closing the net on Simon Cameron. Many times, when we ask God to do something, we expect it to be done our way, but God has His own way of working things out according to His pattern and will.

Chapter Four

The Miracle Happens

It was a Thursday; just another Thursday. Another day of arguments; another day of separation, each one was walking in their own path. My Dad came home for lunch. Something was said, and he blew his top. He ranted and raved, and walked out cursing at Mum. As he left, he roared, "I hate you and I hate your Jesus!" He proceeded to yell that he didn't like the children all that much either, and that he was sick of their marriage. He had had it! "I'll never come back. I don't want to see your face again," he shouted, slamming the door behind him.

Mum had prayed for seven years. She had put up with abuse, she had put up with long nights alone. Her only comfort to help her had been her little daughter's questions about heaven. Now she stood holding her little girl with one hand, and me, a baby in my cot. She had no idea of what to do, and such a sense of failure swept through her being.

Worn and tired, she began to weep. She had never thought she would say these words, but finally in despair she said, "I can't stand him any more." She cried out in prayer, "God, I can't take it. I am going to give him to you." At that exact time, Dad was back at his work. He was now working at a wood factory with his brothers. They had expanded their business from making nets, to manufacturing wooden buildings. Working with a thirty-inch wood saw, he looked at the dust-covered clock and saw that it was three p.m. He didn't know what was about to happen.

Neither did Mum. But God was about to do the unexpected.

Dad looked down at the wood in his hands, trying to concentrate on the end that was approaching the whirling blade. Suddenly, something came over him. He didn't feel right. He shook himself and tried to shrug off this strange feeling. "What's wrong with me?" he thought. He tried to regain his composure. To his amazement he started to tremble. Tears began to stream down his face.

He had heard his brother Michael pray for seven years, "God, save my brother Simon." He had watched his wife pray faithfully and live a godly life before him for seven more years. Fourteen years it had taken for Simon Cameron to come to this point.

He looked at the blurred saw and the wood again. His hands were trembling. Then he realised that his legs, his knees, in fact his whole body was shaking! The tears began to flow as if his heart would break. The dam had burst.

One of his brothers walked past and saw him standing there, transfixed to the spot. He was shaking and trying to fight back tears that nothing could stop. "What's wrong with you Simon?"

In his Scottish dialect, Simon said, "I dinna ken." — "I don't know."

"You'd better go up to the office with me," his brother said. Like a sheep being led, Dad went up and they sat him down on a small sofa. His mother was there, and she made him a cup of strong tea. She knelt down and looked into her boy's face. She had seen him at crisis-points before in his life, but this was different.

"Simon," she pleaded, "what's wrong with you?"

Once again, fighting through the tears and the shaking and the river of emotion, he said, "I don't know. I just don't know."

Then someone suggested, "The best thing we can do is take him home!"

They helped him into the car where he lay down on the back seat. There was no comforting him. They couldn't talk to him, they couldn't reason with him. They eventually decided that he was having a nervous breakdown.

They carried him home, knocked on the door, and Mum opened it. She had every right in the world to turn him away and say, "I don't want him near me ever again. I've suffered enough. He has caused me enough grief and I don't want to see him any more."

She had prayed seven years for this moment, but when she saw him she did not understand what was taking place.

She let them in, and helped Dad to a chair. His brothers explained what had happened, and then left her alone with her husband. Little Wendy was playing outside, and I was still a baby in my crib, just a year old. My mother looked into his face and said, "Simon what's wrong?"

He could only repeat, "I don't know, I don't know!"

And then the Spirit of God begain to move in her heart. "Simon, I think God is beginning to deal with you. I think it's the conviction of the Holy Spirit." He looked at her, incredulously. But instead of the usual violence, silence met her. She gathered up more courage.

"Simon, the Holy Spirit has a hold of you."

Once again, his tears flowed. He was too broken to speak.

Then Mum said, "The Bible says that if you call upon the name of the Lord, Simon, you shall be saved."

Up to this point, Dad had had nothing to do with the Bible. Prayer was revolting to him. He had totally rejected God, and was proud of it.

But when Mum said, "Call upon the Lord," he took it that she meant he had to shout. Through his tears, he lifted his hands and looked heavenward. Through the poverty and drunkenness, through all the doubts and years of bondage that he had known, a hungry heart cried out to God.

"Jesus, tak' me." He spoke in his Scottish dialect, but Jesus is the greatest linguist that man has ever known. Right there and then, a drunk, vile sinner who most people wouldn't dream of visiting, opened his heart, and the King of Glory walked in.

Since then, Simon Peter has said that he can still remember when the first wave of God's forgiveness hit him. I have good news for you, the reader of this book: God has an ocean of forgiveness, and not many days from now, the "anointed moment" is coming for your loved-ones.

Mum had waited seven years for this "anointed moment." Dad had passed from death unto life. It was a surprise, to say the least.

Now Mum realised that the closer he had come to the moment of salvation, the harder he had become. So many times, people have given up praying and believing, when they might literally be one prayer away from breaking hell's power over their loved-one. I know it can be difficult, but the promise is to the overcomer!

Sometimes, God will take people kicking and screaming into the Kingdom of God. That's how it was with Simon Cameron. That day, he poured out his heart to God. He couldn't stop weeping for three days and three nights. All day Friday, all day Saturday and all day Sunday, Simon Cameron wept. He wept his way completely out of his sin and into fellowship with God through Jesus Christ.

I have heard him say since then, that when he opened his eyes after asking Jesus to take him, the lights seeemd to be turned on with double-power electricity. The greens were greener, the blues were bluer, and the reds were redder. Suddenly the burden of his sin had been taken away.

Let me say this — Simon Cameron would never have been saved if someone had said, "Oh, it doesn't matter about sin. God will forgive and just forget about it." Dad knew that his sins needed praying for and needed paying for. It was a bleeding, dying butchered Saviour, hanging on Calvary for his personal sin, that finally broke Simon Cameron. It wasn't damnation preaching. It wasn't the threat of hell or eternal darkness, but it was the love of God that brought him to repentance. It wholly overwhelmed him.

When Dad had been in the world, he was totally consumed by the pleasures of sin. He has said that when he came to Christ, God did not take away the drive or the "want-to" from his life. The Lord just converted it! Simon Cameron came into the Kingdom at ten thousand miles an hour, and he is still going strong today, after thirty years. As he was motivated by God to do great things for Him, Mum had finally seen her prayers answered. In the morning times when they woke, she would glance over to see her sleeping husband, and in his first instants of consciousness, his hands would lift toward heaven. Tears would stream down his face, and a torrent of thanksgiving would flow from his lips towards God for this wonderful salvation.

On the Monday morning after his conversion, Dad got up to go to work. As he left the house, he noticed for the first time that the street which he had walked down every day was lined with trees. The air was cleaner. Everything was more wonderful. The words of an old hymn express the wonder of the experience his heart was now singing about. "Heaven above, a softer blue, Earth beneath a fairer green. Something lives in every hue, Christless eyes have never seen."

As Simon Cameron walked that day, he was still, in material terms, in poverty, but the difference was this — he was changed from the inside! It seemed that the birds in the trees were singing that Simon Cameron had been reconciled to God. From that day on, the world wasn't just improved, it was completely different.

His hunger for God was insatiable. On one occasion, one of the elders of a church came to the new convert and said, "Simon, I know you're excited just now, but it will soon wear off and you'll return to normal." What foolishness! Surely every day with Jesus is sweeter than the day before! It has never worn off yet!

The Miracles Continue

The doctor who had shown such great skill in saving both my mother and myself, during my birth, had a problem which besets many folk, especially, it seems, Scots. He and his wife shared the same "family curse".

Scotland makes money by producing the world's Scotch whiskey, but pays a horrific price for it. Statistics indicate that one in four people who are in mental hospitals in Scotland are there because of alcohol.

My mother always felt grateful to the doctor for her babies, and one day she noticed him in town, looking rather down at the heel. For no reason other than gratitude, and a desire to show Christian kindness, my mother began going down to help in the doctor's house. The doctor and his wife's alcohol problems had brought much hardship. The doctor's house had, in fact, belonged to his mother-in-law, who had bought it to establish him in practice.

Mum would clean that house, get the children ready for school and wash their clothes. With Dad's encouragement, she did all she could to help this family that was being robbed of so much by their alcoholism.

Eventually, everything fell to pieces for the doctor. When his practice collapsed, it was found that he had not been able to pay the mortgage for over a year, and the house reverted back to his mother-in-law. She advertised the house in the newspaper, and there were many prospective buyers interested in the property.

One day, my mother met my father after work. With that familiar smile and look — "Don't ask any questions, just follow" — she said, "Simon I've got the key to our doctor's old house. It's for sale, and we're going down to look at it."

The young man who was making less than twenty dollars a weeks looked at his wife and said, "Wendy, you've got to be kidding. You are joking, aren't you? We don't have enough money to buy the front door handle!"

With that, his red-headed wife smiled and said, "Well, a cat can look at a queen."

They went into the house. My mother knew it well, for she had visited it often. She showed my father around every nook and crannie — there were thirteen rooms in it. Of course, the house was perfect, all and more than they had ever dreamed a house could be.

But all the time Dad was thinking, "This wife of mine is crazy!"

The next day, my mother returned the key to the attorney who was responsible for the sale of the house, and said, "The house is beautiful."

That afternoon the owner went down to the attorney's office and considered the offers that had been made. There were some very handsome offers and she provisionally decided which to accept. The lawyer casually said, "Simon and Wendy Cameron were in and they looked at the house yesterday."

The owner told the attorney to contact my mother and father. He did so, and they were invited to visit her home that evening. The young couple left my sister and I with Aunt Yolande and Uncle Lionel. They got dressed in the finest clothes they could find, and went out to see the owner in her very grand home.

My father looked at the floor, and saw wall-to-wall carpeting for the first time in his life. The fleeting thought passed through his mind that, if he fell, he would never be found again in the thick luxurious pile of the carpet.

She led them into her elegant living room, and they sat down on the fine furniture. They were served tea and biscuits. Then the owner fixed her gaze on the young couple and said, "I hear you have been down looking at my house." Dad's eyes glanced at hers for a moment, and then fell instantly to the floor, embarrassed because he felt he was only wasting this wealthy and important lady's time.

Mum spoke up, "Yes we have, and we loved it. We thought it was beautiful."

The lady spoke to Dad again, "Simon, are you interested in buying the house?"

My Dad looked at Mum and then over to the lady, and answered, "Well, yes, we would like to buy it."

She said, "How much could you afford to give me for the house?" At this point even my Mum wanted to run away.

My father's tongue stuck in his now dry mouth. He was convinced that the next words he spoke were going to be met with a torrent of abuse and insults for such folly. He looked at Mum, did some calculations of the dreams in his mind, and said, "Your house is perfect" (It had thirteen rooms, eighteen-inch granite walls and two-inch solid wood floors. The house was a beautiful mansion). It seemed an eternity as he glanced from Mum again to the lady — then to Mum and back to the lady. Both waited for some profound statement from his lips.

"Well," he coughed, trying to clear his throat. "Well," — a tight feeling came in his chest as he looked down at the floor again, thinking, "I can't tell her the situation, she'll be so annoyed."

"It's all right," she said. "Tell me what you can afford to pay for the house."

"The fact is," said Dad, "the most I can afford (his thickened tongue tried to form words), is eight hundred pounds." (That is worth about

51

twelve hundred dollars today).

With that Mum nearly fell out of the chair. Eight hundred pounds! She had never seen that much money! He continued, "And furthermore (he was finding new strength in the fact that she hadn't passed out at his first statement), we would need you to co-sign for us in order to get a loan."

She looked at Mum and then back to Dad, slowly repeating, "Eight hundred pounds, is that the most you can offer?"

Dad thought, "I knew it. This is crazy. I should never have listened. Wendy should never have talked me into this."

She stood up, and Dad felt he was about to be escorted out of the house.

She fumbled in her pocket, took out a key and said, "Wendy, you have been kind and good to my daughter and my son-in-law. I know about the mornings that you helped get their family ready for school. You've shown a fine example of how a Christian should be."

Stretching her hand out with the key toward Mum, she said, "Wendy, because of your kindness to my daughter and my son-in-law, the house is yours." She passed the key into Mum's hand. She continued, "My lawyer will think I'm crazy, but I don't care. The house was meant for you. Congratulations."

They left her house that evening so excited. Nothing would do except to go down to have another look at it in the evening light. They dedicated the house to the Lord that night. In the years that followed, many people would come to stay there, and many souls came to Christ in that house.

This is by no means the whole story of the Camerons; that will be another book. It is simply the testimony of what God can do for a family. Somehow, in mercy and love, God reached down, looked beyond our faults, and saw our need.

God can use you where you are. First, God used Michael, then Yolande, two young evangelists and finally, my mother. Because of this, I am saved today.

The Bible says, "Lo, children are an heritage of the Lord" (Psalm 127:3). It also states, speaking of a virtuous woman, that "Her children arise up, and call her blessed" (Proverbs 31:28).

Whatever heights my ministry may attain, whatever success any of our family may achieve in this life, we owe it first to God, and second to a young girl who decided to follow Jesus, and who would not be denied! She had lost her baby, and had endured poverty, physical abuse and treatment that would make most people turn their backs in bitterness against God.

Through all of this, one young girl held on to God's promise of Household Salvation. She received the promise. Now, it's time for you to move forward and claim Household Salvation.

Chapter Five

The Reality of Hell

I sat at my desk in the middle of a hectic day. I paused from writing an article and, for just a moment, turned my heart toward God.

It had been two months since God had impressed me with the truth of Household Salvation. I had ministered occasionally on the subject, but felt I had drawn a blank. Half-heartedly, I asked God why this had been the case, little knowing that my short time of prayer would extend through a whole day and night.

In my spirit I heard God speak to me: "I will show you why you don't feel, and why the Church doesn't feel, the reality of the truth of Household Salvation."

Sitting back in my chair, I immediately felt the strong presence of God. Until this time, I had never received a vision from God. In fact, I have always been rather skeptical of such manifestations, and have viewed them warily.

I closed my eyes. Suddenly I saw what I can only describe as a massive conveyer belt on which stood all of mankind. I was there, so were you. We were laughing, playing, working and in general, just living life. There were tiny new-born babies joining our relentless journey. To my amazement, no one seemed to notice the direction in which we were going.

I began to be concerned about where this moving platform was taking us. Suddenly, I saw the end of the journey. It was horrific. Thousands of people were one minute living a normal life, and then the next minute they fell off the edge into an inferno! Their screams and cries were muffled by the roar of the flames that engulfed them. I tried to tell those around me, but the noise of life had made them deaf to my desperate plea.

I began to sob, and then, beyond sobbing, to travail! Suddenly Hell wasn't a distant place that no one speaks of. It was an imminent event, claiming what seemed an innumerable number of people who would never see the light of day again.

I was sick and scared. I didn't want to see any more. This was not the side of eternity that I wanted to experience.

The phone rang, interrupting my thoughts. It was a good friend of mine, so I felt obligated to take the call.

After some pleasantries, she said, "Do you know that seven thousand people die every hour and six thousand of them end up in Hell?" As she finished this devastating statement, her second phone line rang. "I've got to go." With that she hung up and left me with a figure to describe the cascade of souls I had just seen.

I was experiencing real, physical pain at the thought of what I had just seen. I was upset, first at what I had witnessed, and secondly at God for making me feel so uncomfortable.

My mind went back only a few weeks to a situation that had occured in Scotland. A close relative of mine had died in her sins two weeks before I had arrived back home for a short visit. She was buried in a graveyard, which we drove past each day. I casually remarked how the cemetery had enlarged its borders.

"In there," pointed Neil, my brother. "She is buried over there, beside the new wall".

Saddened afresh at the memory, God was about to brutally emphasize His dealings with me. "She is not in that graveyard," I heard the Lord say to me. I felt perturbed in my spirit, half knowing what was coming next. "She is one of the ones you saw falling into Hell."

I did not think I could stand much more of this dealing with God, but He continued, "When you are fifty, she will still be in Hell. When you are seventy, she will still be in Hell. When you have been in Heaven for ten thousand years, she will still be in Hell." I felt physically sick. I had had enough.

"There is no parole from Hell." His words were lethal. "Once lost, once past grace, there is no mercy." My eyes were burning with tears.

In the midst of God's dealings with me, my father had called and heard my wails of agony. He and my mother stayed up all night to pray for me in their home in Scotland. Mother prayed that night, "Whatever you are doing with Philip, Lord, may his pain be for a reason and for Your glory."

I had come, in just a few hours, from wondering why I hadn't seen the response I felt there should have been to my ministry, to knowing without a shadow of a doubt what was wrong. God had to show me Hell, and my loved ones falling over the edge of time, to convince me of the need for Household Salvation. He communed with me again. "Son, most of my Church has lost the urgency to win the lost. That urgency comes from the realisation of eternal Hell. My love has been preached, My provision has been taught, but My justice has been neglected."

I thought shamefully of how long it had been

since I had last spoken of Hell. I, too, was guilty of this sin of omission. That afternoon changed my life forever.

When you remove the judgment of God from the picture, grace and redemption are diluted to mere conveniences, rather than man's most important need.

God's grace would not be needed if there was no such thing as a judgment bar. As the Church faces the greatest test of its existence, preachers are proclaiming the goodness of God and are totally neglecting the severity of God. His goodness was the ark; his severity was the flood. His goodness was shown as the angels warned Lot; His severity was shown in the pillar of salt.

Unless we really realise the necessity for salvation, that an unsaved soul, no matter how much that soul is loved by you or me, will be destined to eternal damnation, we will not be compelled by the Holy Ghost to see them come to Christ.

Instead of silly arguments and banter between the redeemed and the damned, the realisation of impending Hell gives force and power to the believer, who may otherwise be hindered by timidity or pride.

It is the scream of the emergency siren in all of its severity that causes our heart to race, as we steer clear of its desperate rush. We know that someone is in trouble, and for an instant, we too become part of the passing emergency. When one is gripped with approaching Hell, the present becomes precious! TODAY is the day of salvation!

I know this is a terrifying thought, but I must tell you — your husband or wife, son or daughter, mother or father, brother or sister, uncle, aunt, cousin or grandchild is going to be in Hell unless he or she is saved. Your loved-one will fall into a place of total isolation, of outer darkness, where there is weeping and wailing and gnashing of teeth. It is a region of eternal torture, where nothing and no one can help; the land of the damned, cut off from God and from you forever. What do you intend to do about telling them of salvation?

"Soon will the season of rescue be o'er... Soon will they drift to eternity's shore."

In the last thirty years we have gone from giving little thought to earthly comforts, only preparing for Heaven and the sweet by and by, until today when many preachers deal only with the comforts of the sweet here and now. We have gone from one extreme to the other. Once it was thought almost to be a sin to consider oneself as worthy through Jesus' blood. As a boy I remember being told just how wretched and unworthy man was. It crippled any sense of sonship and awareness of the joy our Heavenly Father had in us. All that mattered was, "some golden daybreak." For years the church was beset by such thought.

Today the pendulum has swung to the other extreme. It seems that prosperity is the only priority and faith is used to get ahead in the material aspect of life. How little we hear of the gospel appeal to the sin-burdened heart. I feel that it's time to get things back to the middle ground. Yes, I believe God wants us to be a blessed people, but I also know we must keep our eyes on eternity. I would rather die well, in the knowledge of Household Salvation, than live well a selfish life that would lead to an impoverished death. Instead of, "what must I do to be saved?", the question has become, "What must I do to succeed?" True success and reward is found in a family serving God together in the knowledge of Household Salvation!

Time Is Running Out

After this time of dealing with God, I found myself searching the Scriptures with a new urgency. I was determined to learn all that I could from God's Word about the awful subject of the vision He had shown me.

I wanted to know, not only about Hell itself, but how best to express to my brothers and sisters in Christ, exactly how desperate the situation really is.

My search began in the following verses from Chapter 16 of Luke's Gospel:

"There was a certain rich man, which was clothed in purple and fine linen, and fared sumptuously every day:

"And there was a certain beggar named Lazarus, which was laid at his gate, full of sores,

"And desiring to be fed with the crumbs which fell from the rich man's table: moreover the dogs came and licked his sores.

"And it came to pass that the beggar died, and was carried by the angels into Abraham's bosom: the rich man also died, and was buried;

"And in hell he lifted up his eyes, being in torments, and seeth Abraham afar off, and Lazarus in his bosom.

"And he cried and said, Father Abraham, have mercy on me, and send Lazarus, that he may dip the tip of his finger in water, and cool my tongue; for I am tormented in this flame.

"But Abraham said, Son, remember that thou in thy lifetime receivest thy good things, and likewise Lazarus evil things: but now he is comforted, and thou art tormented.

"And beside all this, between us and you there is a great gulf fixed: so that they which would pass from hence to you cannot: neither can they pass to us, that would come from thence.

"Then he said, I pray thee therefore, father, that thou wouldest send him to my father's house:

"For I have five brethren: that he may testify unto them, lest they also come into this place of torment.

"Abraham saith unto him, They have Moses and the prophets; let them hear them.

"And he said, Nay, father Abraham: but if one went unto them from the dead, they will repent.

"And he said unto him, If they hear not Moses and the prophets, neither will they be persuaded, though one rose from the dead" (Luke 16: 19-31).

What a graphic picture of the agony of eternal torment! The first thing that struck me was the total contrast between the lives that these two men had lived on earth, and their respective situations after death. The rich man in the fine clothes, with an appetite for the finest of foods, left this world for a place where he would have done anything for just one drop of cool water. Lazarus the beggar had known nothing but pain and deprivation in his earthly life, but he had obviously taken care to walk with the Lord. His reward was to be carried by the angels into glorious paradise.

Once more we see how foolish it is to get caught up in those things that are only the temporary benefits of this natural world. If only we would realize that the time we spend here on earth is only the minutest fraction of the eternity for which we are now preparing.

We find the rich man crying out in despair from the midst of the flames that Lazarus be allowed to bring him a little water. Lazarus cannot cross to him however, for we are told that, "there is a great gulf fixed." Hell is final, the separation is irreversible. Once we pass from this scene of time, it will be too late to make changes. It will be too late to rearrange the priorities in our lives.

Worse yet, it will be too late to do anything for our families. Though the rich man's agony is great beyond description, his distress is compounded further by the words which tell him that he cannot warn his five brothers. Not even someone raised from the dead could convince them of the reality of Hell.

Those five brothers would live out their lives, and one day join him in the fire's torment. The rich man's concern for his family is all the more ironic, when we realise that if he had cared just a little bit sooner, he might have been able to do something about it.

Eternity is coming! We ourselves will escape Hell if we have trusted in the saving power of Christ; but what of our loved-ones? What provision are we making for them to join us?

Some people have simply never thought about it. Others just don't care. We MUST care! We MUST pray! We MUST reach them now! We cannot afford to spare any effort if we are to win our families to Christ.

Romans 6:23 is a well-known verse which tells us that, "the wages of sin is death." That "great gulf" we have just read about, is what makes Hell such a tragic fate. For those in Hell will be separated from a loving, caring, God, who is the source of all life and goodness. Hell is death; it is irreversible separation from He who is life. For all of eternity multitudes will know nothing of love, compassion, gentleness, comfort of any of those things that are so vital to life. Such misery is almost too great to contemplate.

Death does not consist of lying quietly under the sod in some peaceful churchyard. For those who die in their sins, it is literally a "lake of fire" (Revelation 21:8). Incidentally, there is a special portion of that fire reserved for liars. The liars I have in mind are those who preach a gospel which is only empty religion, devoid of the power of God and the wonder of life-changing salvation. "You must be born again," the Bible tells us. Those who try to say that we can get by on church membership, and doing good things, and not doing anyone any harm, are lying! If your loved-ones are hoping to reach Heaven that way, it's time to tell them the truth. We may not be able to stop the liars and perpetrators of that kind of false gospel from being cast into the lake of fire, but we can do something about OUR loved-ones.

Almost every time I sit in a church service, I hear someone say, "Jesus is coming soon." It is said so often, that it sails right over the heads of most people who hear it. The fact, though, is undeniable; He is coming soon.

Your theology may lead you to any one of the various viewpoints of how this world will reach its end — but none can deny the fact that there isn't much time left. When the church is raptured, when we, the salt of the earth are gone, the final curtain will be almost ready to fall on the stage of human history. There will be some then who, though alive, will already be condemned to the torture of the Hell we have been talking about.

If this is true — and it is — then time is truly running out for those of our loved-ones who are still not saved. IT'S TIME to discover the promises of God for you and for your house. IT'S TIME to claim the unclaimed promise, and see God do miracles in your family. IT'S TIME for Household Salvation.

I have said much about the reality of Hell because we have to realise just how vital it is for us to win our loved-ones to Christ, but, if Hell is real, then so is Heaven. Only a fool would not want his or her family to share in the glory and joy of spending eternity in the presence of His Majesty, King Jesus. The promise is yours. IT'S TIME TO CLAIM IT NOW.

Chapter Six
Drive Satan From Your Field

I sat once more at my desk, still broken by the vision God had given me. I was haunted by the agony and torment of those multitudes. Each time I thought of my own loved-ones, lost forever, suffering eternal torture — with no remedy, no consolation — I broke down in uncontrollable fits of weeping. My eyes were red and swollen by the flow of the relentless dam-burst of tears. I closed them and tried to compose myself.

"Lord," I prayed, "why are you dealing with me like this? What is it you want me to do?"

Immediately, in my spirit, I saw a large green field. In the field were my loved-ones. I saw my wife and children, my mother, father, sisters and brother, as well as other friends and relatives.

"This is your field," I heard the Lord say. I looked around it. Everyone was happy. Things seemed well. This was a good field and I could be pleased with all I was seeing.

Out of the corner of my eye something seemed to stir. I turned around quickly, but no, there was nothing there, only my loved-ones happily living out their lives. Still, I began to feel uneasy. Something wasn't right. Then I saw him — crouched in the corner of the field, barely visible in the midst of so many busy people. With an evil sneer on his face, Satan looked down at my loved-ones as they lived, loved, dreamed and sought to fulfil all that God had created them to be. I saw him laughing wickedly to himself, seemingly satisfied that all was going his way.

"This is your field," the Lord repeated. "Why have you let him stay in it?"

Then I began to understand something which I need to share with you, and the importance of which you need to realise. In my field I had seen all of those in my sphere of influence. It was my responsibility to cultivate the field. It was my job to sow the seed which would result in the kind of harvest I wanted to reap in my life. Yet in all my busy working, I had made a critical mistake. I had allowed Satan to stay in my field.

The Bible says: "Resist the devil, and he will flee from you" (James 4:7). Many of us have developed the idea that to resist the devil means to spend fifteen minutes every now and then praying and binding Satan's efforts. That's good, but sometimes it's only giving him a little push. It might be enough to cause a temporary imbalance, but it is not resisting him — it is not getting him out of your field.

I'm not a small person, over six feet tall, and no lightweight. If you want to move me anywhere, you had better apply lots of muscle. If we expect to push Satan out of our field, we had better learn to call on the resources of Heaven. Our walk with God, our commitment to a Spirit-led, Word-governed life, all determine how much resistance we are capable of. The weapons are there. The ammunition is available. We have only to keep the lines of communication open to the Commander-in-Chief to know how to mount the attack.

Fifteen minutes of training every now and then does not keep an army fit to repel an enemy. Neither can we expect to deal with the enemy of our souls without a 100 percent commitment to RESISTANCE.

We are blessed in that we know the promise, "Resist . . . and he will flee." But resist we must.

Drive him out, we must. The eternal destiny of those we care for most demands that there be no compromise. Many are content to cultivate their field and then, when they bump into the devil, say, "excuse me," and simply make a detour. No! We must resist him; drive him out in the name of Jesus and in the authority of His Holy Word. We can settle for nothing less than the complete removal of his wicked works from the fields of our lives. What about your field? Will you let him stay or will you relentlessly drive him out?

When we get him out, we must also ensure that he stays out. The devil has no answer to the miracle of salvation. Each one of us who claims Christ as his or her Saviour has the means to be free forever from the power of sin. Yet, the enemy will make every effort to decimate the influence which our lives have on those we love. For this reason we cannot afford to let him sneak back into our field. A little gossip here, a little dishonesty there, a moment of compromise and the field where our loved ones are can be once again at his mercy. RESIST HIM.

Six Rules of Resistance

1. Know Who Is Actually In Charge.

Romans 16:20 tells us: "And the God Of Peace shall bruise Satan under your feet shortly . . ." It is God's power that is able to bruise Satan under our feet. It is not our abilities, or our talents, or anything other than our total dependence on, and commitment to, Him.

The verse says He is the God of Peace. His peace is able to transcend our anxieties and weaknesses and give us the power to crush Satan's skull into the dust.

This portion of Scripture invariably reminds me of that fateful day in the garden of Eden, when God was faced with the rebellion of Adam and Eve. What love He had shown! He had created the world and caused His own light to shine upon it. He had made the heavens and caused the seas and dry land to appear. Then came the sun, the moon and the stars. Birds began to fly, and the oceans were filled with every variety of fish. The earth became home to every living creature.

When all was finally perfect, He made man, the apex of His creation. The first man and woman were without blemish, unique beings formed in the very image of God. In the cool of the evening they would walk and fellowship together, God and man in perfect communion. However, the story soon goes horribly wrong and the Scripture begins to paint a very different picture. Man sins, blatantly rebelling against the authority of God. If you or I had been left to decide what was to happen next, we might well have concluded that it was all a bad mistake. The earth should be obliterated, man destroyed and the whole idea forgotten.

However, the God of Peace had something to say to the devil: "And I will put enmity between thee and the woman, and between thy seed and her seed; it shall bruise thy head; and thou shalt bruise his heel" (Genesis 3:15). What unfathomable love! When He would have been justified in blotting out man forever, He makes the first monumental promise of a coming Messiah who would cancel the power of sin for all time.

From the very beginning of Scripture we are shown who it is who can keep the devil out of our field. Jesus, living in us, will bruise Satan's head and thwart his evil plans for us and our loved-ones.

The last word of Romans 16:20 is, "shortly." God wants us to get Satan out of our field immediately! There is no reason, no good one that is, for delay. IT'S TIME – to lift up our foot, bruise Satan's head, and drive him out of our field in the name of Jesus!

2. Prepare For Total Effort.

"I beseech you therefore brethren, by the mercies of God, that ye present your bodies a living sacrifice, holy, acceptable unto God, which is your reasonable service" (Romans 12:1).

God is no longer interested in the sacrifices of animals on the altar. Instead, He is interested in living sacrifices! It is a spiritual fact that we can have as much of the power of God operating in our lives as we are willing to make room for. If we want more of God, then some other things may have to go.

We cannot afford to retain anything which prevents us from keeping God in the place of pre-eminence in our lives. Sometimes it isn't just the bad things that have to go. God will sometimes require of us that we put Him before those things which most people would regard as their "right."

Matthew 20:28 reads, "The Son of Man came not to be ministered unto, but to minister . . .". If Jesus came into this world, realising that he had to serve on a level of continual selflessness, should we expect anything different for ourselves? The servant cannot be greater than his Lord. God will bless us, and supply all our needs, but we must realise that it is a case of, "first things first".

I am reminded of a testimony I once heard. A particular brother was very wealthy and owned vast herds of cattle. Each day he would walk around his property and say, "Lord, these are your cows."

One day, while doing this, God spoke to him. "Son," the Lord said, "I want you to sell these cows and put the money into the mission field."

"But, Lord," the man replied, "you know that this is the wrong time. The market is bad. I won't sell them now. I just can't."

"Whose cows did you say they were?" asked the Lord.

Somewhat sheepishly, our brother began to realise that these were not God's cows, after all, and that he had been only kidding himself. He had just gone through the motions paying only lip-service to God's demand for "living sacrifices."

Our possessions, our time and our talents have all been entrusted to us by God. He wants us to be stewards unto Him (I Corinthians 4:2), and to be ready to invest all of our resources into His Kingdom.

We can't forget the fight for a moment. We have to be ready to win our loved-ones at any cost!

3. Prepare to Pray

Moving on from the Scripture which we have just discussed, we find in verse twelve of the same chapter, a glorious theme which is often proclaimed in the Word of God. We are instructed to be ". . . continuing instant in prayer." So many of us would rather worry, sweat, fuss and fume, instead of turning first to the power-house of prayer.

How many times have you been under pressure about something? Perhaps you've lost an important document that simply has to be found immediately. You'll turn the house upside down and you'll get mad at everyone, whether or not they could have been remotely involved in the document's loss. Then, in a final desperate moment you turn to the Lord for help. You flop down wearily into a chair, only to discover that you have just sat on the elusive piece of paper. "Next time, Lord," you promise, "I'll make sure I come to you first."

The only problem is, many of us go through the exact same routine every time. Even when the difficulty is much more serious than a lost piece of paper, we still so often keep prayer as some sort of last resort. The Scripture says, ". . . continuing INSTANT in prayer."

At the first sign of Satan's attempts to get back in your field, go to prayer. Each time someone in your field, in your sphere of influence, is a target of Satans's dirty tricks, pray, pray, and don't stop praying, till God gives you the answer. Each time you feel the pull towards something that would try to displace the total Lordship of Jesus Christ in your life, pray until you touch the heart of God. Pray through, until God's spirit sweeps through your being, and you receive an infusion of divine strength and power.

The old hymn says, "Can we find a friend so faithful, who will all our sorrows share? We should never be discouraged, take it to the Lord in prayer." We must remain instant in prayer if we are to have any hope of resisting the devil effectively. We can drive him out of our field forever, through effectual, fervent prayer.

4. If You Don't Want To Get Burned, Don't Play With Fire.

Coming back to Romans chapter sixteen, this time to verse nineteen, we are given the instructions which directly leads to having the ability spoken of in verse twenty, to bruise Satan's head: ". . . I would have you to be wise unto that which is good, and simple concerning evil."

It has been rightly said that Satan quakes every time he meets a Christian who knows how to use the authority of the name of Jesus. Yet some of us underestimate him. In our own human strength, Satan has nothing to fear from us. Many people think that it is possible to dabble with the devil and then pull out with no ill effect. That kind of thinking can get you into desperate trouble. Someone has said, "If you are going to sup with the devil, you had better use a long-handled spoon."

God is telling us to be simple concerning evil. For instance, I am blessed in that I came to Christ when I was just four years old. I have never been inside a bar, and I wouldn't know what to do if I were in one. I know that many have been wonderfully delivered from alcohol, including my Dad, but I thank God that I have never known the problem. That is one type of evil about which I can state that I am blissfully ignorant, or simple. However, if I were to wander down to the nearest saloon and start to observe and participate, I could be in over my head and bound up in no time by the same curse of alcoholism which has plagued the Camerons for generations.

People who have been delivered from something usually know enough to keep away, but sometimes there are others who just feel the urge to "try it and see." It doesn't have to be alcoholism. Often people are simply blinded. They fail to see behind the facade of the bright lights, and end up snared by the world's fatal attractions. This is why we need to keep out of dangerous territory and why we need to avoid contact with those who dance to the world's tune. We certainly need to witness to them, but in no way can we live by the rules they set.

The answer, of course, is to concentrate on being "wise unto that which is good." What we think about or talk about, what we read, watch, or listen to, will all determine how effectively we will be able to respond when faced with a spiritual battle. If we feed our spirit on an uplifting diet of positive, Word-centred "food" we can be sure of internal solidity and strength.

Those who feed the mind only on what comes out of the television set are going to have a much harder time finding motivation and determination when things start to get rough. This is a whole subject in itself, and does not need to be dealt with further here, but the importance of this fact is paramount to our successful Christian walk. In order to drive the devil out of your field, in order to resist him, we must dwell on what is godly and good. If we do not, we will find ourselves wandering too close to Satan's territory. It may well result in our testimony being ruined and our loved-ones lost for all time. RESIST HIM. DRIVE HIM OUT OF YOUR FIELD — NOW.

5. Operate By The Rules.

The rules are God's immutable principles, as laid down in His Word. The following verses provide a good starting point:

"Be not deceived; God is not mocked: for whatsoever a man soweth, that shall he also reap.

"For he that soweth to his flesh shall of the flesh reap corruption; but he that soweth to the Spirit, shall of the Spirit reap life everlasting.

"And let us not be weary in well-doing: for in due season we shall reap, if we faint not" (Galatians 6:7-9).

Some have taken the principle of sowing and reaping and make it into some kind of magic formula for gaining riches. However, the financial side is only a small part of it. It is certainly true that God rewards faithfulness in the area of giving, and that He is no man's debtor; but there is much more. We cannot trigger God's blessing just by dropping a few dollars into the offering plate. If we give to get, then God is not being glorified. However, when our heart's desire is to be a channel of blessing to others, then miracles become possible.

Seed The Need

You do not need to be a farmer to know that in order to reap barley, you must sow barley. It would be silly to sow one thing and expect to reap another. An old verse says, "There is a law that runs through life, You gather what you sow — You cannot plant a thistle, and expect a rose to grow." I believe that you can "seed the need." If healing is your need, then begin to pray for those in your church or area who need to be healed. I don't mean just pray a quick prayer. I mean seek God in a genuine and selfless way. You are reading this book because you want your loved-ones to come to Christ. Perhaps you should begin to reach out to families in your area with the Gospel message, and minister to someone else's loved-ones. "Seed the need," and you set in motion God's unchangeable law of sowing and reaping.

We have already said that what you feed your mind affects your spiritual effectiveness. This is also sowing and reaping. If you sow good seed in your inner man, you will reap a harvest of strength of character, motivation and stability.

This portion of Scripture tells us to "be not weary in well doing," and to "faint not." You may wait a long time for harvest time to come around. Things may be getting desperate in the situations you face, but keep sowing — the harvest is on its way! It might seem easier to give up and look for some short-cut which might conveniently happen along. But if it means compromise, if it means sowing bad seed, then leave the short-cuts to the others. "Faint not" is just another way of saying RESIST. If we determine in our hearts to live by the Word of God and to sow "to the Spirit," we will be equipping ourselves with exactly the right requirements to resist the enemy and to keep him out our field. "He that soweth to the Spirit shall of the Spirit reap life everlasting." That's life everlasting for you, and for everyone in your field!

6. Prepare For A Fight

In case you are still in any doubt, I am telling you how to fight a war. Not only do you need to know how to fight, but you need to realise that you will actually have to get involved in the battle itself. Once you decide to resist the devil, he is going to come out fighting.

When Joshua was being commissioned to lead the children of Israel into Canaan, he is told four times in Joshua Chapter One to "be strong and of a good courage." Now that chapter is full of promises for prosperity, success, blessing and so on. But although Joshua was assured of the continuing presence of God — "As I was with Moses, so I will be with thee; I will not fail thee, nor forsake thee" (Joshua 1:5), he still had to have the courage to look the enemy in the eye. He still had to fight his way through no less than three major military campaigns.

Yes, God is with us. Yes, we can depend on His strength. But we alone make the choice whether or not to face the enemy in battle.

With so much at stake, with the fate of our loved-ones hanging in the balance, we must fight ceaselessly against the wicked one. We need to look him in the eye and do battle! We must resist him in the name of Jesus, and totally remove his influence from our field.

It will also pay you not to forget that you are fighting a master tactician. Satan will use every trick in the book to get to you and those you care for. However his tactics are of no effect against the wisdom and sovereign power of God. So keep those communication lines open. Keep praying and pressing on toward your goal of total Household Salvation. The promise is yours! You'll have to fight, you'll have to give it total effort. It will take perseverance and sowing good seed. You will need to be instant in prayer, and you won't be able to fool around in the devil's territory. But one day, you'll survey your field, and all around you will be your loved-ones, praising and magnifying God. Satan won't be there because he'll know he's lost the battle for your field. Victory is on its way for you! The salvation of your family is on its way — it could happen any time now! RESIST HIM! DRIVE HIM OUT NOW — AND WATCH GOD DO MIRACLES FOR YOU.

Chapter Seven

The Promise Of Household Salvation

I have shared with you the miraculous way in which God transformed the Cameron family. His sovereign power brought our whole family into a marvellous relationship with Him, but there is something which you must understand here. There was nothing special about the Camerons, except perhaps a huge appetite for sin. There was no logical reason on earth why God should have moved in our family. He simply took us as we were, and loved us, and poured out His life changing grace in our lives.

The Scripture says: ". . . God is no respecter of persons" (Acts 10:34). I believe with all my heart that what God did in our family, He is more than willing to do in yours. The first thing we must establish is that God's Word has put the issue beyond all doubt — Household Salvation has been promised to you! We must know this promise and we must claim it and live our lives in expectancy of the day when everyone in our family will be rejoicing in this wonder of full salvation. IT'S TIME FOR HOUSEHOLD SALVATION.

Read carefully these verses of Scripture:

"Speak ye unto all the congregation of Israel, saying, In the tenth day of this month they shall take to them every man a lamb, according to the house of their fathers, a lamb for an house:

"And if the household be too little for the lamb, let him and his neighbour next unto his house take it according to the number of the souls: every man according to his eating shall make your count for the lamb.

76

"Your lamb shall be without blemish, a male of the first year: Ye shall take it out from the sheep, or from the goats:

"And ye shall keep it up until the fourteenth day of the same month: and the whole assembly of the congregation of Israel shall kill it in the evening.

"And they shall take of the blood, and strike it on the two side posts and on the upper door post of the houses, wherein they shall eat.

"And they shall eat the flesh in that night, roast with fire, and unleavened bread: and with bitter herbs they shall eat it.

"Eat not of it raw, nor sodden at all with water, but roast with fire; his head with his legs, and with the purtenance thereof.

"And ye shall let nothing of it remain until the morning; and that which remaineth of it until the morning ye shall burn with fire.

"And thus shall ye eat it; with your loins girded, your shoes on your feet, and your staff in your hand; and ye shall eat it in haste: it is the LORD's passover.

"For I will pass through the land of Egypt this night, and will smite all the first born in the land of Egypt, both man and beast; and against all the gods of Egypt I will execute judgment: I am the Lord.

"And the blood shall be to you for a token upon the houses where ye are: and when I see the blood, I will pass over you, and the plague shall not be upon you to destroy you when I smite the land of Egypt." (Exodus 12:3-13).

Here we read of the origins of the Jewish feast of Passover. Moses had been raised up by God to deliver the children of Israel out of their bondage to the Egyptians. Time after time God had performed mighty signs and wonders through Moses to show Pharaoh that God was moving on behalf of Israel. But Pharaoh refused to listen, for the Lord had hardened his heart, and he would not let the children of Israel go free. So Moses delivered his warning from God that judgment was on its way. An angel of death would come. He would slay all of the first-born in every house. The only ones who would escape this awsome fate would be the children of Israel; but even they would only escape if they followed the Lord's instruction to the letter.

They were to take a lamb, kill it, and with a bunch of hyssop dipped in the lamb's blood, they were to strike the lintel and doorposts of their houses. This is the term which was used, and it thrills my heart every time I read it: " A lamb for an house."

Once the blood had been spread on the lintel and doorposts of that house, every single individual inside that home would be safe when the death angel passed over.

"When I see the blood," the Bible says, "I will pass over you, and plague shall not be upon you to destroy you."

Can't you see it? If the blood of an ordinary lamb was enough to ensure safety for an entire household under the old dispensation, how much more will the blood of the Lamb of God, shed on Calvary, make provision for salvation for you and your house.

Back in Chapter Ten of Exodus, Moses said something wonderful. Pharaoh had tried to get Moses to leave Egypt with only the men-folk. Finally he tried to get the children of Israel to leave behind all of their cattle. But Moses was determined that every man, woman, boy, girl, and even their livestock, would march triumphantly out of Egypt. "There shall not an hoof be left behind" (Exodus 10:26).

Oh, that Christians today would be similarly determined that not one single member of our families will be left in the devil's kingdom. We can take them all to Glory with us, if we begin to accept and claim God's promise of Household Salvation.

Rahab the Harlot –
The Woman Who Saved Her Household

Rahab may have been known as a harlot, but she was in fact a woman who proved to be determined to bring the blessing of God upon her entire household. Her story in Joshua Chapter Two is one of the most moving examples of God's response to simple faith in Him.

Joshua was about to lead the children of Israel into the Promised Land. Standing as the prime obstacle to the fulfilment of all their dreams was the walled, fortress-like city of Jericho. The "City of Palms," they called it. As a strategic city where three of the main ancient trading routes converged, its capture was vital to the progress of the children of Israel into the Promised Land.

Its thirty-foot high double-walls stood in awesome defiance of any prospective attacker. This was going to be no easy task; the outer wall was six feet thick and the inner was twelve feet thick. A miracle was needed — and the Lord began to arrange circumstances to prepare for exactly that.

Joshua sent two spies into Jericho to assess the enemy's strength. Somehow the spies were spotted and the king of Jericho sent his soldiers to capture them from the house where they had taken lodgings — the house of Rahab the harlot.

Rahab, instead of turning the men over, as one might have expected her to do in response to a command from no less a person than the king himself, hid them on the roof of her house. Carefully, she covered the men with stalks of flax. Some of those stalks had been over a yard long and up to an inch in diameter, so a few well-placed bundles would have afforded a perfect hiding place.

When the soldiers arrived, she told them that the men had been with her but that they had since left. "Pursue after them quickly, for ye shall overtake them," she said misleading the king's soldiers.

You might be asking yourself why she took such a risk. The answer to that question is found in verse nine:

"And she said unto the men, I know that the Lord hath given you the land, and that your terror is fallen upon us, and that all the inhabitants of the land do faint because of you."

Rahab was simply aware that if God was moving on behalf of these people, then there was nothing anyone could do to stop them. She also realized a judgement day was coming. Rahab's later rescue can be directly attributed to the fact that she believed God, while the others in the city did not. Her faith was such that it merits her inclusion in God's "Hall of Faith" in Hebrews Chapter Eleven. She continues to show this faith to the two spies by saying ". . . for the Lord your God, He is God in Heaven above, and in earth beneath (Joshua 2:11).

Simon and Wendy Cameron on their wedding day.

Simon and friend in the army.

This is where Michael Cameron found Christ.

Simon's baptism in 1956.

Simon street preaching in Peterhead, Scotland in 1962.

This was Philip's first trip to the
United Sates 1969.

The entire Simon Cameron family.

New Hope; Scotland's first Spirit filled
Bible College and Missions training centre.

Philip Cameron at the phone set during
a live "100 Huntley Street" telecast.

The Philip Cameron family, Philip, Chrissie,
Philip Aaron and Melody Joy.

Rahab boldly extracted a promise from the two spies, that in return for the kindness she had shown them, they would save alive her father's house when they returned with the armies of Israel to destroy Jericho: ". . . save alive my father, and my mother, and my brethren, and my sisters, and all that they have, and deliver our lives from death" (Joshua 2:13).

What a marvellous example of how we should feel about our families' salvation. Rahab was absolutely determined that every single person connected with her would be saved. Later in Chapter Six, when we read of the capture of Jericho, we find that Joshua indeed saved Rahab and "her father's household, and all that she had" (Joshua 6:25).

The little house must have been packed to the ceiling with Rahab's loved-ones. It may be that many of them had not loved her, but we are not asked to pray only for those who love us, but for those who despitefully use us.

As a sign whereby the armies of Israel would know Rahab's house, she was to tie, from her window, the scarlet cord that she had used to let the spies down from her rooftop. That scarlet cord speaks to us of the blood of our Saviour, still freely flowing, still availing for sin, and still able to secure salvation for you and your house.

Can you imagine the scene? Rahab scurrying around trying to persuade her family to come to her house. She had been sworn to secrecy, so she could not tell them what they were needed for. It is quite conceivable that there were some members of Rahab's family who weren't even on speaking terms with their "harlot" relative. But black sheep or not, Rahab threatened, begged and cajoled her family into coming to her house. Remember also, that she had no idea how long it would be until the Israelites would come. Her little house must have been packed tight with people from the moment the spies left.

A woman who had compromised every moral fibre of her being, changed both her priorities and her lifestyle in order to accommodate the many members of her family whom she wanted saved.

Rahab could have asked those two spies for anything. She was talking to people who could soon control the city and all its riches, but she had no thought for gold or fine garments. Her only concern was for the saving of her household.

Rahab was saved and lived the rest of her days with the children of Israel. The Scripture tells us that she married a man name Salmon (Matthew 1:5). Tradition has it that he was one of those same two spies who came to Jericho. Reading in Matthew Chapter One, we find that Salmon and Rahab are in the direct lineage of the One who would provide the means of salvation for every household.

Rahab — a harlot and a Gentile — through her determined faith in the God of Israel, not only saved her entire household, but became an earthly ancestor of the Saviour of the world — Jesus Christ.

With God on your side, anything can happen. Your background doesn't matter, neither does the enormity of the problem you face. What matters is the depth of your trust in the Lord God, who is God in heaven above and in earth beneath.

Can God save your family? Of course He can! Is He interested? Does He care about you and yours? Of course He does! The God who can take a harlot and place her in the royal lineage of the

King of Kings, can take you and bless you with full Household Salvation — IT'S TIME!

Noah – The Man Who Prepared An Ark To The Saving Of His Household

Hebrews 11:7 reads: "By faith Noah, being warned of God of things not seen as yet, moved with fear, prepared an ark to the saving of his house . . .".

I'm sure that we are all familiar with the story of Noah and the ark, but it bears mentioning here, because again we are brought face to face with God's desire that all of us should be concerned with our household. Not only that, but we are shown what it is that motivated Noah. In fact, it also motivated Moses and Rahab in their particular situations.

Noah was moved with fear. His fear was born out of the knowledge that something was soon to occur for which he had to prepare his family. Moses knew it was coming, and so did Rahab. What was it? It was judgment! It is all very wonderful for preachers and teachers to minister about the goodness of God and all His many blessings, but we cannot afford to forget the other side of the coin. The Scripture says: "Behold therefore the goodness and severity of God . . ." (Romans 11:22).

We must never forget that God's judgment is real, and if we do not win our loved-ones to Christ, then they will have to face that judgment. The final judgment for sin is Hell, and at that point all the joking stops. I have already shared with you how God left me in no doubt as to the savage reality of the fate of those who die in their sins. We do not have time to waste! We must reach our loved-ones for Christ — NOW! IT IS TIME.

One of the most graphic statements I have ever read is found in Genesis 7:16; "And the Lord shut him in." It wasn't Noah who shut the door of the ark, it was God who shut the door. Noah had stood for righteousness in the midst of a perverse generation. All the time that Noah had been building the ark, the people had opportunity to repent and turn to God. But when the moment came, when God finally decided that it was time for judgment, He closed the door to His mercy and all of mankind except those in the ark were destroyed.

We must face the fact that God's judgment is again going to come upon this earth. That's why my watchword has become, "IT'S TIME." It isn't just a slogan, a nice logo for people to recognise our ministry by. It is a truth of which I become more aware with every passing day. IT'S TIME — FOR HOUSEHOLD SALVATION.

It's Time To Prepare An Ark For The Saving Of Our House

One of the great privileges of my life has been the opportunity of co-founding, with my father, "New Hope Bible College and Missionary Training Centre" in Peterhead, Scotland. It is not only a Bible college. It provides headquarters for a host of our outreach ministries that, I pray, will one day touch every household in my homeland of Scotland.

Not only have we had the joy of leading others to Christ, but we have put, right in our own back-yard, an ark for the saving of our house. Every one of my immediate family — my mother, my father, and the four children — are involved in full-time ministry through the work at New Hope. Many of my relatives are part of New Hope Church, or other nearby churches, and have experienced salvation directly as a result of New Hope evangelism programs.

You may not need to build a Bible college, or sponsor a nation-wide outreach ministry, but where you are, you must have a part in preparing an ark for the saving of your house.

If we were fully aware of the extent of the tragic judgment to come, we would not rest until every member of our family was safely in the ark of God's salvation. We have to do all we can — IT'S TIME.

Household Salvation in the Book of Acts

The theme of Household Salvation runs right through the New Testament. One of the places where it comes through strongly is the book in which we read of God laying the foundations of His church.

In the book of Acts we see numerous thrilling instances of God showing us that salvation is not only for us alone, but also for our household.

In Acts 11:13,14 we read, ". . . call for Simon, whose surname is Peter; who shall tell thee words, whereby thou and all thy house shall be saved." In a strange sort of way, I feel a bit like that. God has shown me to tell people everywhere, words whereby they and all their house shall be saved.

I want to make sure that you understand that the words which you are reading on these pages are more than just nice writings about some good idea. It is much more than a good idea, it is a God idea – God wants you to be saved, and your house.

Further on, in Acts 16:14, we are introduced to Lydia. We are told that she is a woman whose heart the Lord opened and that she attended unto the things which were spoken of Paul. The following verse tells us that this results in her being baptised, and her household. In the same chapter, Paul and Silas are gloriously visited by the power of God while in prison. Their bands are loosed. The jailer rushing in, begins to attempt to commit suicide, thinking that the prisoners had escaped. Paul cries out to him, "Do thyself no harm: for we are all here."

Falling down before Paul and Silas, he asks that most marvellous of questions: "Sirs, what must I do to be saved?"

Paul's answer is one which has thrilled the souls of men and women ever since it was spoken: "Believe on the Lord Jesus Christ, and thou shalt be saved, and thy house" (Acts 16:31).

The story continues: "And they spoke unto him the Word of the Lord, and to all that were in his house. And he took them the same hour of the night, and washed their stripes; and was baptised, he and all his, straightway" (verses 32,33).

What a wonderful salvation this is! God's heart of love is not content to stop at your life alone being changed and blessed by His power. He won't rest until He gets you to realise that you can see your whole family share in the marvel of redemption. IT'S TIME for Household Salvation.

It's Your Right

This must be made completely clear; I am not just telling you that it is possible for your family to be saved. I am telling you that it is your God-given right to expect salvation for your whole household. I have shown you how God did it in my family and I have shown you what the Word of God has to say to you about it. There is not room for argument. Household Salvation has been promised to you. It is your right.

The reason that many of our loved ones are still unsaved is because we have not claimed the promise; we have not directed our faith toward God on behalf of our families.

I should point out here that I am not suggesting that you embark on a campaign of nagging and badgering your relatives to receive salvation. That wouldn't help you or them. But by living a godly life before them, even when they abuse you, and by fully expecting by faith that God will move to bring them in, things will begin to happen. God will turn the situation around.

When life begins to deal its hard blows, you had better be ready for them to come to you for the help they need.

God will show you opportunities beyond your imagination to prove to them His power working in your life. It works! IT'S TIME for you to see it work for you! Household Salvation is your right!

We have seen from the Scriptures how God has made Household Salvation part of the package for every Christian. As you read on, I intend to show you some of the specific things that you can do to make it a reality in your life. I pray that you have already begun to realise that God is, even now, moving on your behalf.

You have already begun the process whereby God will bring them in. If you are willing to trust God and believe His Word, then you can be truly sure that IT'S TIME — for Household Salvation.

Chapter Eight

Here's What You Can Do

From what we have discovered so far, we can see a plan emerging which, if we will follow, will cause us to take giant steps forward to bringing our entire families to Christ.

Let us look further at the processes involved in achieving Household Salvation.

1. Resist The Devil And Drive Him From The Field Of Your Life.

We have gone into this in some detail, but we should realise that there is much more to defeating Satan than just reading a few pages in a book. You can put a book on the shelf and forget about it. However, you cannot afford to leave valuable knowledge on a shelf; you must use it effectively. All the learning in the world will do us no good whatsoever if we do not incorporate it into the practicalities of everyday life. Therefore, it is not just enough to agree that we should resist the devil, we must ensure that next time we have to deal with him, we actually do resist him.

Most people will nod their head readily in agreement with the steps to resisting Satan which we have discussed. They will say "amen" to such propositions as knowing it is God who is in control, or giving total effort to the fight, or continuing instant in prayer, but we must do more than agree; we must ACT! If we really are serious about wanting to bring our families to the Lord, we are going to have to be certain that we form the daily habitual process of making sure that Satan is driven from our field.

I cannot emphasize this enough. Resisting Satan

needs more than good intentions or the mental acceptance of some "magic formula." It needs action – conscious, deliberate action. Neither the intention or the desire to resist Satan will budge him one inch, but when you actually take authority over him by the power of the Holy Spirit in you, and resist him in the name of Jesus, he will FLEE.

2. Be Aware of Impending Judgment

If we forget the reality of Hell, and that its torment awaits those of our loved-ones who die in their sins, we will lose our motivation to win them to the Lord. Rahab knew that judgment was coming to Jericho and it prompted her to move into action to save her household. Noah was "moved with fear" and he built an ark to the saving of his house.

We have two things which we must never forget. One is that Hell is real and the other is that the end of this age is imminent. We need to burn those facts into our minds every day. Just as we cannot forget to resist the devil, neither can we forget the horror and irrevocability of a sentence to eternal damnation.

Again, however, we need more than mere words. It is action we need. Ask yourself every day, "Am I doing all I can with this day's opportunities to ensure that my loved-ones don't end up in Hell?"

3. Claim The Unclaimed Promise

When we begin to resist the devil, we will soon discover the value of prayer. If we intend to see our families come to Christ, we must begin immediately to pull down the strongholds of Satan through an active and determined prayer life.

As we pray, our faith will be encouraged greatly as we rejoice in the promises of God's Word concerning our household. We need to absorb these promises into our spirit and begin to claim them for ourselves. God's promise is to you! What you must do is begin to live as though you believe it! One key factor here is an overcoming perseverance which refuses to stop praying and refuses to stop believing, despite situations which may even appear to be growing worse.

My mother prayed for seven years — that's a long time to pray. My father's determination to break her grew stronger by the day, but he didn't break mother, God broke him.

My aunt Chrissie, who was saved on that same marvellous evening with my mother, was married to a man named Charlie. She prayed for him for over twenty years. Like my Dad, Charlie would fly off the handle every time Chrissie mentioned Jesus. One day, after he had been quite ill for some time, Chrissie looked at him as he sat in his chair. He appeared somehow to be distressed. She thought, "I would love to ask him just one more time if he would like to be saved, but I know it will just cause a scene."

Then Chrissie heard the voice of the Lord speak softly to her: "Go on, ask him just one more time." So Chrissie knelt down by the side of Charlie's chair and did as the Lord had told her.

"Charlie," she said, "don't you think it's time you got saved?"

Tears immediately began to stream down Charlie's face. "Oh Chrissie," he sobbed, "I thought you would never ask."

Charlie, who had been so hard and hostile, wept his way to Calvary and was transformed by the love of God.

Chrissie could have given up, she could have

said, "No, I don't want to risk another argument," but she knew the voice of God and she knew the promise of God. God moved in Chrissie's impossible situation and He certainly can move in yours.

Remember, don't give up believing. Don't give up praying and claiming your promise. It's always too soon to quit!

I also believe that while we need to persevere and win our families — whatever it takes — God is about to do a quick work.

Through our television and radio ministry, people have been calling and writing in prayer requests for their unsaved loved-ones from all over the U.S.A. and Canada. Some of them have been praying about their family members for a number of years, yet it seems so many have discovered that their very act of faith, in writing or calling, has been the catalyst for miracles in their lives.

Amazingly, some people were calling back to us within hours of their first call for prayer, to say that God had supernaturally saved their loved-ones.

It can happen for you, so begin to believe it. Claim that promise now. IT'S TIME!

4. Let God Do It His Way.

We humans have an incredible tendency to interfere with things that are none of our business. I am certainly not saying that the salvation of our household is none of our business, but how God brings it to pass is dependent on His wisdom, not ours.

My son Philip is six years old. A couple of years ago, he went through a stage which , I supposed, all little boys go through. He wanted to do everything by himself and prove his independence and ability. Even in the simple matter of combing his hair, he was determined to make sure he lent a hand. I would try to comb his hair and his hands would be everywhere trying to help. Eventually, I would get to where I had to pin his arms to his sides by holding him between my knees, and then quickly do the job.

Invariably, he would wriggle one hand free, and just as I was almost finished he would say, "Me do it, Daddy." A little hand would shoot up like lightning, finding its way to his hair, where he would begin to "comb" with his fingers.

Somehow, I think God must face the same problem with us. Just as He is getting ready to do what we have prayed so hard for, we decide to lend a hand. Like the famous bull in a china shop, we barge into things that would work out so much better if we would just leave it to the Lord. We don't help matters one bit by nagging. For instance, if an unsaved husband is drinking, perhaps a wife might find herself plunging into despair because, "Oh, dear, he's drinking again."

Certainly, it isn't good news that he's drinking again, but it isn't going to help anything if we get depressed and lose our faith-grip on God's promises, or if we "pitch a holy fit" and start lecturing him about what a bad boy he's been. He is acting that way because he is unsaved. He does not understand the need to conform to the standards of a spiritual life. If you nag and fuss, you may create a bigger problem because of the barrier of resentment which can be built up. It is, of course, necessary to be there, to love, to advise and, through the life you lead, to show the way to a better answer than can be found from a bottle or anything else.

Just to set the record straight, let me say that men can be pretty good too when it comes to nagging. If you don't believe me, ask my wife! I'm joking a little, but please don't miss the point.

I believe that if we will concentrate on our walk with God, and present a Christianity which is real, and not some ethereal, mystical, far-away-look-in-the-eyes religion, we can get through to our loved-ones in a much more effective fashion.

God knows exactly the circumstances we are in. None of our difficulties take Him by surprise. When He wants to move upon the hearts of your loved-ones, He will enter right into their situation. He will speak to them clearly in their own terms, in a way which will leave them in no doubt about His love and power.

When the Lord told Peter to launch out into the deep and to let down his nets, all Peter's instincts told him it was folly (Luke 5:3,11). He had been working all night long. He was a fisherman. He knew every good fishing spot in the region. Yet, all of his experience had been to no effect. How could this stranger, this carpenter's son, know more than he? Didn't he know that you don't catch fish in the daytime? Nevertheless, he obeyed — and Peter and his men collected so many fish that they filled two boats to the point that they were in danger of sinking.

Nothing could have spoken to Peter more clearly than this. He knew that only Divine forces could have caused this miracle, and brought so many fish to where there had been none the whole night long.

The miracle's immediate effect on Peter was to convict him of his sin. "Depart from me; for I am a sinful man, O Lord," he said (Luke 5:8).

From that point, Peter became a disciple of the Lord Jesus, and he was never the same again. I believe with all my heart that God is just as able to get right down to where your loved-ones are living, and talk to them in their own language. God will show them just as clearly that He can move mightily in their particular circumstances.

What we have to do is to watch for the "special, anointed moment," and be ready to act, just as Chrissie was when the Lord spoke to her to "ask just one more time."

Let God do the job His way! You can't alter the situation by worrying, by fretting or by fussing. We can alter it by praying, by believing and by trusting God to keep His promise of HOUSEHOLD SALVATION.

5. Let The Nature Of God Motivate You.

We must understand that God's heart of love is such that it is His desire to save every single member of our families.

He will bless you because of your very concern for your household. When Lot was rescued out of Sodom, it wasn't because of anything that Lot himself had done. It was because of faithful Abraham's forceful intercession. Lot was rescued, but Abraham's blessings were innumerable. He learned how to commune with God and walk into the knowledge of the power of prayer. He became the "Father of the faithful."

It should go without saying, that God is displeased when we fail to take up our scriptural responsibilities in respect of our family. The Word of God says: "But if any provide not for his own, and specially for those of his own house, he hath denied the faith, and is worse than an infidel" (I Timothy 5:8). These are strong words indeed.

94

"Your Concern Is Only
A Fraction Of My Concern"

My father tells of an incident that happened to him as he was travelling one day by car near Los Angeles. His brother, Alex, was driving, so Dad took the opportunity to have a time of inward meditation and prayer. As he did so, he began to think of some of our relatives back in Scotland who had still not come to Christ.

He began to pray, "Lord, I'm so worried about my family. It hurts me to hear of them still bound by sin." Some of them were, in fact, often to be seen staggering down the street in a drunken and near-paralytic state. "Lord," he continued, "I'm so concerned about my household."

Dad began to feel the Spirit of the Lord move upon his heart and say to him, "Son, you have said that you are concerned about YOUR household, but I want you to know that your concern is only a fraction of my concern. If you are concerned about YOUR household, know that I am concerned about MY household, and I am working now to move upon their hearts."

Whenever your heart begins to be touched by the spiritual need of your family, you also touch the heart of God. His very nature is to love, save and transform.

The nature of God can be seen in the reaction of Jesus to the cries of Mary and Martha. They mourned the loss of Lazarus — one of their house. At the same time, they expressed great faith: "Lord, if thou hadst been here, my brother had not died" (John 11:32).

The reaction of Jesus? He wept. He was so involved in this family situation, so touched by the love of Mary and Martha for their brother that He wept. He not only wept, He raised Lazarus from the dead.

If you have not realised it — Jesus cares for you, and He cares for your family. He cares enough to promise you that if you remain faithful to Him, He will save your entire household.

The nature of God is such that you can move Him, because your concern evokes His concern, your love evokes His love — and His love will change your family!

Taking this thought just a step further, we should take the time every now and then to marvel at the wonder of the character and nature of our Lord. In Isaiah we read:

"Behold, my servant shall deal prudently, he shall be exalted and extolled, and be very high.

"As many as were *astonied* at thee — His visage was so marred more than any man, and His form more than the sons of men.

"So shall He sprinkle many nations; the kings shall shut their mouths at Him: for that which had not been told them shall they see; and that which they had not heard, shall they consider."

The word used in verse 14 is "astonied." It is an old fashioned word, meaning ASTONISHED. The prophet is trying to tell us something. — The nature of Christ is so marvellous, so indescribably wonderful, that it is simply ASTONISHING. If we want our loved-ones to fall in love with Jesus, we can never afford to lose our sense of astonishment at the lovely Nazarene.

He is so astonishing, we read here, that kings shut their mouths at Him. He is so astonishing, that whenever He came to town, He put all the doctors out of business. The Bible says, "He healed them all" (Matthew 12:15).

He is so astonishing that He could die on the cross, and turn death and seeming defeat into the very means of life and victory for all mankind.

He is so astonishing that He could promise, "Believe on the Lord Jesus Christ, and thou shalt be saved, — AND THY HOUSE" (Act 16:31).

So be astonished; be enraptured by the person of Christ. Be willing to let Him turn your concern for your family into the blessing of a closer walk with Him for you, and the miracle of Household Salvation upon all of your household. Let the nature of God motivate you!

6. Know The Promise.

Below, I have simply listed some key Scriptures to help you believe for Household Salvation. I know that you will come across many more in your own studies. However, these will form a good starting point:

Deuteronomy 7:9: "Know therefore that the Lord thy God, He is God, the faithful God, which keepeth covenant and mercy with them that love Him and keep His commandments to a thousand generations."

Hebrews 6:17: "God also bound Himself with an oath, so that those He promised to help would be perfectly sure and never need to wonder whether He might change His plans (Living Bible)."

Proverbs 13:22: "A good man leaveth an inheritance to his children's children: and the wealth of the sinner is laid up for the just."

Isaiah 54:13: "And all thy children shall be taught of the Lord; and great shall be the peace of Your children."

II Corinthians 1:20: "For all the promises of God in Him are yea, and in Him Amen, unto the glory of God by us."

Psalm 103:17,18: "But the loving kindness of the Lord is from everlasting to everlasting, to those who reverence Him; His salvation is to children's children of those who are faithful to His covenant and remember to obey Him (Living Bible)."

Jeremiah 2:9: "But I will not give you up — I will plead for you to return to me, and will keep on pleading; even with your children's children in the years to come! (Living Bible)."

I Samuel 2:35: "Then will I raise up a faithful priest who will serve me and do whatever I tell him to do. I will bless his descendants, and his family shall be priests to my kings forever. (Living Bible)."

Acts 10:2: "A devout man, and one that feared God WITH ALL HIS HOUSE, which gave much alms to the people, and prayed to God always."

Acts 16:31: ". . . Believe on the Lord Jesus Christ, and thou shalt be saved, and thy house."

Luke 19:9: "And Jesus said unto him, 'This day is salvation come to this house, forsomuch as he also is a son of Abraham.'"

Luke 8:39: "Return to thine own house, and show how great things God hath done unto thee: And he went his way, and published throughout the whole city, how great things Jesus had done unto him."

Exodus 12:3: "Speak ye unto all the congregation of Israel, saying, 'In the tenth day of this month they shall take to them every man a lamb, according to the house of their fathers, a lamb for an house.'"

Acts 11:13,14: ". . . Call for Simon, whose surname is Peter; Who shall tell thee words, whereby thou and all they house shall be saved."

Acts 16:14,15: "And a certain woman named Lydia, a seller of purple, of the city of Thyatira, which worshipped God, heard us: whose heart the Lord opened, that she attended unto the things which were spoken of Paul. And when she was baptised, and her household, she besought us saying, If ye have judged me to be faithful to the Lord, come into my house and abide there. And she constrained us."

This chapter does not deal with everything you can do about achieving Household Salvation, but if you will put these principles into practice in your life, I am convinced that you will set in motion the forces of Heaven to work on your behalf. And remember — IT'S TIME.

Chapter Nine

Mothers – God's Secret Weapon

One of God's secret weapons in His plan to bring Household Salvation to the church is the praying, Bible-believing mother, who refuses to let the devil get hold of her children.

I speak very much from experience here. I could not begin to think where I would be today if my mother had not been the kind of woman who wanted, above all else, to see her family living for God.

They say that the most valuable evidence in a court room is that provided by an eye witness. I am not writing this because it seems to be a good theory, or because I have heard someone else share a message which seems to fit into my ministry. I am writing this as a personal testimony to the awesome difference that a godly mother makes to a family situation.

As a young boy, I would often decide what I wanted to be when I grew up. Sometimes it was a pilot, or train driver, or a fireman, depending on what took my fancy at the time.

"That's good," my mother would say when I told her. "But let me tell you about someone."

She would then proceed to tell me stories of great men of God down through history. Each time I would reply by saying something like, "That's right, Mum, when I grow up, I'm going to a preacher like my Dad." Mum made sure that all of my heroes were preachers, and none greater than my Dad.

I recall one time when I had traded some bubble gum cards for a poster of Jimi Hendrix, one of the big rock stars of the day. In my childish excitement, I took the poster home and ran up to my room. Carefully, I pinned my new treasure onto the old chipboard wall of my bedroom.

"Mum, come and look at this," I shouted down the stairs to her. When she came into the room, I began to enthuse about the talents of my new idol. For a moment there was silence. Then she spoke softly (how I would come to dread it when she spoke to me in that soft voice), "I wonder how many young people he'll be responsible for sending to Hell? If you want to leave the poster there, you can — the choice is yours. Your Dad is away preaching right now, winning people to Jesus. I don't think the man in the picture will ever do that. Do you?" With that she left.

I stood there more stunned than if she had yelled at me and given me a sound thrashing. Looking at the poster on the wall, I began to get angry at myself for getting so wrapped up in someone whose only achievement in life was he could play a guitar. I tore the poster from the wall and ran downstairs. "Throw it in the garbage can, Mum," I said. "I don't want anything to do with it."

The Most Exciting Place In Town

Mum turned our house into the place where everyone wanted to be. When I would meet my friends and suggest that we go somewhere, they would invariably say, "No, let's go to your house instead." She turned our backyard into the most exciting place in town.

If we played football, she played football. If we did anything at all, she was right in the thick of it with us. She couldn't swim, but she took us to the pool and taught every one of us to swim. She taught me to box and to ride a bike.

Once, my cousin John and I decided to dig a hole all the way from our backyard, which was going to end up, according to our calculations, in Australia. Being Scottish, we would then, of course, charge a suitable fee to those who wanted to use our hole to take this amazing shortcut to the other side of the world. Needless to say, it wasn't very long before tired muscles got the better of us and we abandoned the project.

While we were resting from our labours, we decided to lay a trap for anyone who might have wanted to sabotage our hole. So we perched a bucket of water above the door which led into the backyard.

You can imagine the sickening feeling which gripped my stomach when who should come through the door, but my mother. Down came the water and the bucket on top of her, just missing her head and drenching her to the skin.

For just a moment, she looked surprised and bewildered, then her eyes seemed to say, "Wait till I find out who did that." Then, seeing our horror stricken faces, she began to fall into uncontrollable fits of laughter.

Somewhat relieved, we began to laugh too until we were rolling on the ground in danger of falling into our newly dug hole.

On another occasion my cousins, my sister and I built ourselves a little camp in the backyard. We had an old pear tree which grew out at the oddest of angles from the back wall of the yard. By carefully draping an old tarpaulin across the branches, we made ourselves a little shelter and packed it with everything we could fit into it. We had chairs, mattresses, and what we thought were all the comforts of home. Our plan was to spend the night there, but when it began to pour with rain, we decided to "camp" on the floor of one of the rooms of the house instead. On the way out I knocked one of the candles, which we were using for light, onto one of the straw mattresses on the floor. I picked up the candle, blew it out and folded over the mattress, thinking I had taken care of the problem.

After we had settled down on the floor of our indoor camp-site, my mother came in. "Did you kids put out the candles under the tarpaulin?" she asked.

"Yes Mum," I replied with confidence.

"Well, come and see this."

We followed her out into the yard to be greeted by the sight of our carefully constructed camp, now a roaring inferno, billowing forth columns of thick, black smoke. What followed was another one of those hilarious slapstick situations that had to be seen to be believed.

We tried to form a chain to carry buckets of water to put out the fire. One of my aunts preferred to run around with a little jug, spilling most of the water as she ran. Mayhem is not the word for it. It is honestly a miracle that we didn't burn the whole street down.

Faith Adventures

Sometimes things took on a more serious note. When Dad was away preaching, Mum would often be pressed to make ends meet. However, she turned everything into an adventure, and time after time, God would meet our need in an amazing way.

We took in boarders to try to help provide income to supplement the meager funds which

Dad was able to bring back from the tiny offerings he received.

Sometimes we would be literally down to nothing. There would be no food whatsoever in the house, and supper time would be coming on fast. Somehow, Mum never felt or showed anxiety.

She calmly said, "Let's pray together. Lord, you know we are in need. Send someone to us now." I could not count the times that a knock would come on the door almost before we finished praying.

Mum would go to the door. "Do you have a room?" she would be asked. The boarder would, of course, pay in advance, sometimes for several nights at a time. Mum would give me some of the money and I would run around to the little store just around the corner from our house, and dash back with enough food for supper for us and our boarder. I would pass the supplies through the kitchen window and Mum would go about the job of making supper as if nothing had happened. She somehow just knew it would come.

As a little boy, I saw faith in God work for our daily needs, and as I have grown, so has my faith. We had never lacked a meal. God was always on time. Some of our greatest blessings were the folk God brought to us in that way.

The Rabbit Lesson

One day my Dad brought home a pet rabbit from one of his preaching trips. I could not have wished for anything better. Rabbits were the latest craze to hit our school and everyone, it seemed, had their own rabbit.

Well, now I had the rabbit, but I had nowhere to keep it.

"Mum," I asked "can we buy a rabbit's hutch?"

"Son," she replied, "You know that we don't have much money. We just couldn't afford that right now." I begged, pleaded, yelled and tried everything to get her to say yes, but to no avail.

Finally, in a childish tantrum, I cried, "It isn't fair that I can't have it just because Dad wants to go away and preach. Everyone else can afford their own rabbit's hutch." With that I slammed the door and went off to bed to sulk.

Next morning I got up and went down to the kitchen, hardly remembering my temper of the night before. I wasn't ready for the sight which awaited me when I opened the kitchen door. Mum had fallen asleep, crouching over something on the floor. In one hand was an axe; she had been using the blunt end as a hammer. Underneath her was a newly finished rabbit's hutch, which she had just spent the whole night making out of small fruit boxes.

She woke with a start. By now I was in tears as I realised the trouble she had gone to, just to make sure that her boy wouldn't be able to say that he had to do without something because his Dad was a preacher.

"This is for you Philip," she said. I couldn't say anything as I realised how selfish I had been, and yet another spiritual lesson was etched into my heart.

A New Guitar

As I grew older I wanted to learn to play an instrument, so Mum bought me an old, cheap guitar. Today, I can play several instruments without too much difficulty, but it was a different story then. In fact, there were those who assured her that I had no ear for music and that I should forget trying to play anything.

However, I had inherited a good-sized streak of determination and I persisted with my dream. "The day you can play a hymn on that guitar which I can recognise," my Mum promised, "I'll buy you a good guitar." That was all I needed.

I did have one problem, though. The neck of the guitar she had given me was just too big for my fingers to get around to play it properly, so I had to come up with something fast. Where I got the inspiration for the idea I came up with next, I do not know. I somehow managed to lift out the magnifying glass from the gauge of a set of bath-room scales. By placing the guitar on my knees, and using the glass, I was able to play the guitar "Hawaiian" style. Eventually I mastered a tune and I proudly called in my Mum and Dad and played to them 'The Old Rugged Cross'. Mum knew that a promise is a promise, and she assured me that I would get my guitar.

I will never forget the day they took me through to the music shop in Aberdeen to buy my new guitar. They made me wait in our old van while they went into the shop. What I didn't know then was that the guitar cost thirty-two pounds and they had only sixteen. So they had gone in first to avoid embarrassment in front of me, because they did not know if the shop would approve them for credit or not. I remember crying with excitement as they brought the guitar out to me. The guitar cost my parents what, at that time, was a small fortune. The sacrifice, when I think of it now, was immense, but my Mum and Dad would never grudge anything that could be used for the Lord's

work. No money was ever spent on wordly entertainment, but all we had could be spent on God.

A Mother's Wisdom

Over the years I've discovered something about
my Mum. She is the closest thing to omniscient
that you will ever meet in any human being. So
many times as a child I would do something
wrong, and before I even got home, she knew
about it. She would just speak to me in that soft
voice. I would cry out to her, "Smack me. Yell at
me, but please don't talk to me in your soft voice."

Nowadays, I'm more grateful for her wisdom.
I'm glad that, without saying a word, she knows
what I'm thinking and when I'm hurting. If I need
straightening out, though I'm no longer a little
boy, she knows exactly how to do it.

There is a saying, "The hand that rocks the
cradle, rules the world." Mothers, the role you
play in shaping your children for God could not
be more vital.

I am only one of four children, all of whom are
full-time in the Lord's work, and we can all tell our
own stories of how Mum moulded us and directed
our desires toward God.

So often, in modern society, the role of the
mother is treated with disdain. Women are made
to feel inadequate unless they go out and "do
their own thing."

I cannot help but think that no one could
achieve anything more satisfying or worthy of
greater honour than bringing up their children to
know the power of God moving in their lives.

My mother used to pray, "Lord, I do not ask
you for beauty, or for wealth, or for nice clothes,

or any of those things. All I ask is that you allow me to bring my childen up to serve you." She would ask God to so mark us with Himself that we would radiate Christ without being asked. "What's the point," she would say, "of going through the pain of giving birth (and she knew that only too well), of struggling to bring up your kids, only to hand them over to the devil when they grow up?"

You only need to own one small precious jewel to guard it carefully. How much more a child's life?

Many nights I would hear my mother praying by my bedside that God would cause me to grow up to serve Him. My head would be turned away. She wouldn't know I was awake and I would hear her weep for me before the Lord. I used to lie there with tears flowing down my cheeks, knowing that I could never be anything but what she prayed for me to be.

If you ever meet Wendy Cameron, you will know instantly that I haven't even begun to tell her story. God often uses Mum in the gift of healing. She knows what it is to minister under the anointing of God before thousands of people. Yet, when you talk to her, you will find that it won't be long before she begins to talk about her kids, and how the most important job of her life has been to create in them a hunger for God.

Mothers, you are God's secret weapon. You can alter the course of history by the way you yield to God when bringing up your children. The world needs more men and women of God. Whether or not the Lord gets them early in life might well depend on mothers who know how to listen to God, and "train up a child in the way that he should go." For then, the Bible says, "when he is old, he will not depart from it." (Proverbs 22:6). My mother set her heart and mind on Christ and geared everything in that direction. Her constant prayer was that God would lead her.

Saved By A Mother's Love

In the Scriptures we find that the vital role of the mother is emphasized time after time. My mind turns to the story of Moses, starting in Exodus Chapter One. The decree had gone out: ". . . every son that is born ye shall cast into the river . . ." (Exodus 1:22). Surrounded by the screams of mothers as they saw their children drown before their eyes, a mother and daughter desperately planned a way of saving their son and brother. Other mothers had just given up and accepted the seemingly inevitable. This mother had decided to attempt to thwart Pharaoh's plan.

Meticulously, they prepared the tiny ark, making sure that every gap between the reeds was filled with pitch. Diligently they laboured, even as death's hand fell all around them. God was on their side, and during the construction of the little craft, not one soldier approached their dwelling. You see, they were working according to the will of God.

How they managed to carry their precious burden to the river one will never know, but I have found that faith creates its own opportunities.

At the water, they placed the child in the ark. His mother went back to labour as a slave, manufacturing bricks for Pharaoh. The sister stood silent vigil over her brother, against what seemed impossible odds.

When she saw the princess and her entourage

approach the location where her brother was, Miriam could have panicked, done the wrong thing, and caused death to come upon her entire family. Instead, she hid until the opportune moment. Swallowing her fear, the little slave girl approached the princess. With a courage that only love can give, and by deft negotiating, she not only saved her brother, but created a paying job for her mother to bring up Moses.

I repeat that one of the greatest weapons in all the world is a mother's love. Hell cannot stop a praying, believing mother from achieving her aim when she has decided to claim the promise of Household Salvation.

They never knew what Moses' call would be. They just loved this baby and refused to see him die. Today we know of Moses as the man who saw more miracles, apart from Jesus, than any other man. But when he was helpless, a mother stood in the gap; a sister refused to let her brother be lost.

Mothers, as Hell claims its six thousands souls per hour, I want you to stand up and proclaim that none of your seed — no loved-one of yours — will be lost. With a determination from God, withstand the power of Hell. By the power of the Blood of the Lamb, and the word of your testimony, witness God move and bring them in.

Hannah Prays For A Son

The Bible clearly shows that if you dedicate your children to God, the future can be filled with wonder. Those children can grow to know the blessing and power of God moving in their lives in ways that can surpass your highest dreams.

Elkanah's wife was Hannah. His other wife,

Peninnah, had children, but Hannah was barren. We find the heart-broken woman grieving in the temple, crushed by the cruelty of Peninnah's taunting insults. She was so deeply wounded that she couldn't even bring herself to speak her pleas aloud to God.

The old priest saw her moving her lips, but no sound came out. "She's drunk," thought Eli.

Hannah was not drunk. Rather, she had been swept away into intimate communion with God, and she made a vow: "O Lord of hosts, if thou wilt indeed look on the affliction of thine handmaid . . . but wilt give unto thine handmaid, a manchild, then I will give unto the Lord all the days of his life . . ." (I Samuel 1.11).

She declared that no razor would ever come near his head, signifying that this child would be of the order of the Nazarite. Like Samson before him, Hannah's child would be set apart, kept from strong drink and uncleanness, and wholly given over as one of God's special vessels. God answered the cry of Hannah's heart and gave her a son.

We can tell this story so glibly, and not fully appreciate the courage of character shown by Hannah. It was no easy thing to give Samuel over to Eli the priest. She knew that once it was done, she would have no more say in her son's future.

Nevertheless, she kept her bargain with God and handed Samuel over, not really sure of what would become of him. We know that her faithfulness resulted in the emergence of a mighty prophet who would guide the children of Israel as the oracle of God.

That baby in your arms today, that tiny, helpless

bundle, has a potential in God. Guide, mould, pray, teach and show, and God's boundless resources and power will flow to and through that child.

The choice? It's yours! "Choose life that thou and thy seed may live" (Deuteronomy 30:19).

Chapter Ten

Fathers

If the role of the mother is vital, it is all the more crucial that the father knows how to play his part in bringing his family to the experience of full Household Salvation. The mother's hands are so often tied by a father who refuses to fulfil his spiritual obligations within the family structure. Often, for apparently good and honourable, but nonetheless mistaken reasons, fathers can do irreparable damage to their children's zeal toward God.

More money, a better job, a bigger home, comfort and plentiful provision for the family might sound like the best motivational forces for a father, but that can be a wrong, and sometimes fatal, misconception. My father would never allow money or possessions to come between God and his children.

The book of Ruth tells of a man named Elimelech. His name means "God is King". His wife was called Naomi, meaning "pleasantness".

This family man had two sons named Mahlon and Chilion. Scholarly opinion differs as to the meaning of their names, but I feel that the meanings, "a song" and "a sense of completeness", paint the most accurate picture of the situation which Scripture is describing.

That's quite a family setting! God is the King, in overall charge of the household. Pleasantness rules the home, and daily life is accompanied by a song and a sense of completeness. What is more, they live in Bethleham-Judah — "the House of Bread."

This idyllic scene is not to last, however, as a famine sweeps across Israel. Elimelech begins to be saddened by his own hunger and that of his family. He starts to wonder how to improve the situation and ensure that his family suffers no further.

Elimelech's first fatal error was in failing to realize that the difficulties they were facing were the consequences of spiritual, and not natural, problems. God had made absolutely clear His determination to lovingly provide for the children of Israel: "...If thou shalt hearken diligently unto the voice of the Lord ...and... do all His commandments... the Lord shall make thee plenteous in goods... (Deuteronomy 28:1 and 11). "But... if thou wilt not hearken unto the voice of the Lord... the fruit of they land... shall a nation which thou knowest not eat up." (Deuteronomy 28:13 and 33).

There could only be one reason for famine in Israel: disobedience to God, and rebellion against His sacred Word. That never seemed to strike Elimelech as he desperately considered his options. Finally, he decided on a plan. He would leave the House of Bread and journey, with his family, to a place called Moab. Possibly, in his time of deliberation, he had climbed into the high country around Bethlehem. From there he would have been able to see the plush, green pastures of Moab in the distance, and he decided that his future lay there.

There was only one difficulty with Elimelech's plan. Moab means, "the land of no father". The Moabites were direct descendants of the children conceived by the incestuous relationship which the two daughters of Lot contrived to have with their father (Genesis 19:31-38). The very name "Moab" was anathema in Israel, and the law specifically forbade the entering of a Moabite into the congregation of the Lord (Deuteronomy 23:3). For Elimelech even to entertain the thought of going to Moab, was a sign of unspeakable spiritual backsliding.

Fathers, you are the ones who so often determine your family's future by the decisions you make. In God's name, don't ever make a decision based on income, without first considering the outcome.

Elimelech led his family on the journey away from the House of Bread, little knowing the tragedy that lay ahead. But then, tragedy goes hand in hand with decisions that take you out of the will of God.

The route taken by the family very probably led them close to the still ruined walls of the city of Jericho.

"What happened here father?" I can hear one of Elimelech's sons asking.

"Oh, this is where God did a mighty miracle when our forefathers first came to this land. God caused the walls to fall down and He delivered the city into the hands of the children of Israel."

"Why doesn't God do miracles now father? Why has He stopped doing mighty wonders for Israel?"

No answer.

A little later, they would find themselves passing the two piles of memorial stones, one at Gilgal, and the other close by at the River Jordan. "And these father, what are these for?" the other son might have asked.

"These were erected to commemorate the day that the Lord stopped the flow of the River Jordan when it was swollen with the spring floods. God allowed the children of Israel to pass across Jordan on dry land."

"God must have done many miracles, father. Why doesn't He do them now?"

Again, no answer from Elimelech.

Eventually, the family reached Moab. They tried to settle down and just live like everyone else in Moab. The two sons even married Moabitish girls.

One day, Elimelech died. When you deliberately wander from God's will, you can be sure that it won't be long till the sense of God being King dies within your bosom. Soon to follow were the deaths of Mahlon and Chilion. The song had died; the sense of completeness was replaced by tragic emptiness.

The message could not be more clear. If, as fathers, you make decisions based only on materialistic ambitions or on an overriding concern for this world's treasures, you will be courting disaster. I cannot count the times I have heard my father earnestly pray, "Lord, I don't care if I have to live in a tent, just make sure my family are all serving you." His one desire is for all his children to work full-time for God, and for nothing with his blood to be left behind.

My father is anything but perfect, but I know him better than anyone on earth, and I know that when he prays like that, it isn't empty words.

If you want your family to rise up on the streets of glory one day and call you blessed, don't get your priorities mixed up now. If a better job takes you away from the fellowship of the saints, let them keep it. If a certain deal means compromising your Christian integrity, run from it. Those little eyes are watching. They may not say a word, but you will never fool them.

"I'll Take What Daddy Takes"

I'm reminded of the story of a young boy whose mother had to be away one day. This meant that the little fellow had to spend the day at the office with Dad. The young boy occupied himself in a quiet corner while Dad took care of the day's business.

Lunchtime came and Dad said, "Let's go for something to eat son." Proudly, the young boy set off with his dad; so pleased to be sharing this special day. Dad was the hero of his life, and this was a day he would always remember.

At the restaurant, the waitress came to take their order. "What will you have sir?" she asked.

"Just the usual thank you," replied the business man.

"And for you?" she asked the boy.

"Oh, I'll take what Daddy takes," he beamed.

"What will you have to drink, sir?" she queried, meaning an alcoholic beverage.

Uncomfortably, the man looked at his son for a moment, then quickly answered: "Just the usual."

"What will you have son?" the waitress asked.

The little boy smiled trustingly at his father, and again replied, "I'll take what Daddy takes."

The stark truth is that children all over the world have found themselves ending up in trouble, because all their lives they said, "I'll take what Daddy takes."

What are you taking Daddy?

I know that this might be said of mothers too, but I am talking right now to the decision maker, the head of the home. If you don't decide for God, you may be condemning your children to a life of despair and an eternity in Hell. No double standards can be allowed. Many children end up hopelessly confused, because what their parents say is often vastly different from what they do.

In the book of Joshua we read of a man named Achan who "took of the accursed thing." He disobeyed a direct command of the Lord and brought chaos into the camp of Israel. When the crime was discovered, he was taken away and stoned to death. Not only was he stoned, but so were his wife and his children. Everyone and everything connected to him was destroyed. In the lists of geneologies in the book of First Chronicles (I Chronicles 2:7), the line of that particular house comes to an abrupt end with the name Achan.

There is no getting away from it — the decisions of fathers will have effects on their families which will stand for eternity. Whether the effects are bad or good depends on how the decisions are made. Ask yourself: "Will it glorify God? Would Jesus do it? Is it in accordance with what the Bible says? Does it hurt anyone? Will my family's spiritual life be impaired?"

Let those questions have precedence over, how much will I make? Will I have a better house, a newer car, a fancy office?

Read Exodus 20:5 for a sobering thought: "...I the Lord am a jealous God, visiting the iniquity of the fathers upon the children unto the third and fourth generation of them that hate me."

If you lapse into sin, please don't be so foolish as to think that it's your problem, and no one else's business. What you do will affect you, your wife, your children, and perhaps your descendants, for years and years to come.

I have not even addressed the many other horrendous possibilities of temptation to which fathers are uniquely vulnerable; but the stakes here are higher than every fortune on earth put together. The souls of your children and loved-ones are hanging in the balance! There really is not a choice. It has to be God first.

Fathers, you must do everything possible to ensure that Christ is the reason for living in your home. It is your responsibility to ensure that everything you do as a family revolves around the person of Christ. When your kids see you unashamedly living for Christ, and displaying a deep, intimate love relationship with Him, then they will be irrevocably influenced towards God.

Mothers and fathers sometimes fight with each other, or let each other and their children down in various ways. No one can expect you to be perfect — but you can be real. My parents don't always agree, but I've seen the laughter at the end of an argument, which makes us children laugh as well.

Your children will not be taken in by religion that makes you all smiles in church and a brute at home. Oh, won't you let Christ invade every part of your life? Give Him more of yourself each day, so that even when mistakes are made, your children will see your honest efforts to get things right. Let them witness that the value you place on walking with God is greater than any passing disagreement or mistake.

The promise of Household Salvation is yours, and no one can take it away. Even the devil cannot take it away. Receive it! Walk in it! Live it! IT'S TIME!

Chapter Eleven

God is Never Late

I have made much use in this book of the phrase, "IT'S TIME". I want now to show you from the Scriptures that God is always on time. He is never late, and no matter how bleak things look at the moment, help is already on the way.

You may be reading this book and not fully concentrating on it because your mind is consumed with worry over some loved-one dear to you. Perhaps an unsaved husband is breaking your heart; or a teenage son or daughter is out on the town tonight, seeking pleasure, but risking disaster. Or it could be your wife who refuses to countenance the life you are leading, preferring to try to live a life without Christ.

Whatever your situation, I want you to take courage, because IT'S TIME for God to move in your life.

My father lived an un-godly life, and for seven years and put my mother through hell while he was at it. It seemed that things were never going to get better. The more my mother prayed for him to get saved, the worse he got. Finally, when it seemed that she could not go any further, when all hope was gone, God changed the whole situation around in one afternoon. Mum often says she discovered that God's permanent address is "Wits-End Corner". She was at the end of herself, but God was only just beginning to execute His purposes — in the course of His precise and perfect timing. He is never late! He knows the beginning from the end and He is the master-planner of the ages.

My mind turns to the story of Jonah, known by many as "the Reluctant Prophet." God had given him instructions to go to Ninevah and preach repentance to the city, but Jonah ran from the calling of God and booked himself passage on a ship. A great storm arose and the ship's crew decided that Jonah was the cause of their troubles.

The Scripture says: "So they took up Jonah, and cast him forth into the sea . . ." (Jonah 1:15). Think of it for a moment. Poor old Jonah is out in the middle of the sea. There is a fearsome storm raging and he's just been thrown into the ocean from the boat. His only hope of ever seeing dry land again was sailing away.

The Bible says in Jeremiah: "Behold, I am the Lord, the God of all flesh: is there anything too hard for me?" (Jeremiah 32:27).

All flesh includes whale flesh and I can hear the instructions going out to that whale as it swam the ocean depths. "Get yourself to these precise co-ordinates. Be near the surface and be there at the exact time I specify — don't be late! A man is going to drop into the sea and I want you to swallow him, but you make sure you don't chew him!"

Sounds crazy, doesn't it? But the story goes on: "Swim the three-day journey to the beach at Nineveh (How does a whale know where Ninevah is?), swim onto the dry land (not something you find whales doing very often), and spew out the contents of your stomach on the beach."

I can't tell you how God did it. I only know that He did, and that Jonah made it to Ninevah, even if he was slightly the worse for wear. The poor fellow would have been sucked pure white by the whale's gastric juices and his hair would have been full of seaweed and fish bones. Little wonder that he had such a powerful impact on the awestruck Ninevites when he pushed his white little finger in front of their faces and gurgled "Repent!"

God is never late! It was time for Jonah and it was time for Ninevah. When God wanted to accomplish His purposes, He let no obstacle, no whale, no storm, no reluctant prophet stand in His way.

Another incident involving a fish happened when the tax collectors came looking for the apostle Peter (Matthew 17:24-27). The Lord told Peter to go down and cast in his hook and that the first fish to come up would have enough money in its mouth to pay their taxes. Even Peter, in all of his impetuousness, must have felt a little strange carrying out that command. Can you see that little fish swimming to the sea bed, picking up a coin of the exact value needed and then coming up toward the surface to look for Peter's hook? The fish had to be sure that it didn't get on to anyone else's hook. It had to be the right one. Beloved, God has always been on time, and in the matter of your family's salvation, He will be on time yet again.

What stirred in the hearts of the animals to cause them to make their way towards rescue in Noah's Ark? It is quite conceivable that the distances which some had to travel meant that they would have to reproduce, before dying on the way, and let their young keep the appointment at the little wooden boat. If God can control the forces of nature in such a miraculous way, can we seriously doubt His ability to save our loved-ones?

One of the most fascinating examples in Scripture of God's perfect planning and timing is to be found in the book of Esther. Two apparently unrelated events occur which later prove to be cruicial in the unfolding plan of God. The first incident took place as the result of a drunken party in the palace of Ahasuerus, king of Persia. This king is identified in secular history as a despotic tyrant, who thought nothing of executing people for the slightest deviation from his wishes.

In his drunken state, the king ordered his beautiful queen, Vashti, to show herself before his guests. This was apparently intended to be a lewd and immodest display. The queen refused and the king was left looking rather foolish before the assembled dignitaries. The king's counsellors put pressure on him to make an example of the queen and he weakly agreed, and issued a decree removing her from her royal position. The vacancy created was filled by the lovely Esther, after an arranging of circumstances which only God could have performed. Esther was a Jewess but that fact was hidden until much later.

Esther's guardian, Mordecai, then found himself involved in an incident which seemingly, was quite separate from the events which had taken place up until then. Mordecai overheard a plot to assassinate the king and duly reported it, allowing for the capture of the would-be assassins. We are told nothing more of the incident except that it was recorded in the national records.

Then, on the scene, appeared a man named Haman, a wicked, egotistical man, hungry for power. Haman was given a position of prime-ministerial importance and the inhabitants of the land were commanded to bow in his presence. However, Mordecai the Jew refused to bow, indicating his determination to bow to no one but to no one but to the God of Israel. The inflamed Haman then contrived a plan to convince the king that the Jews were his enemies and, once again, the king was swayed into issuing a decree. This time the order was for the total annihilation of the Jewish people. Decrees made by the Persian kings were irrevocable, so the situation for the Jews was critical and desperate.

In one of the most wonderful passages in all of Scripture, Mordecai sends for Queen Esther. As a Jewess, she would also suffer death if her origins were discovered. Esther is told that she must go before the king and plead for the lives of the Jewish people. That, however, was a dangerous task in itself, since the penalty for going unbidden into the king's presence was death. Mordecai assured Esther of the necessity of taking the risk and spoke some strong words to her: "For if thou altogether holdest thy peace at this time, then shall there enlargement and deliverance arise to the Jews from another place: but thou and thy father's house shall be destroyed . . ." (Esther 4:14).

This verse continues with a question that you can ask yourself in your situation, as you believe God for your loved-ones to be saved: "Who knoweth whether thou art come into the kingdom for such a time as this?"

The situation was desperate. The total destruction of the Jewish nation was imminent unless something totally miraculous took place. That miraculous something was about to happen because of the boldness and faith of a little Jewish girl whom God had caused to become a queen.

After three days of fasting, Esther made her brave entrance into the presence of the unpredictable king. Mercifully, he stretched his sceptre towards her, signifying that she would not be punished for this breach of court etiquette. It is a fact that serving God can often put us in some very uncomfortable, unpredicatable and even dangerous situations, but the spiritual destiny of so many souls may depend on our willingness to take the risk.

Esther's fortitude resulted in her being put into a position to incriminate the evil Haman. At the same time, Mordecai's previous service in saving the king's life was amazingly and miraculously brought to the king's remembrance. Mordecai was honoured and Haman was hung on the very gallows which he had prepared for Mordecai. The Jews were given authority to defend themselves against anyone seeking to do them harm which, in effect, nullified the decree ordering their destruction.

The situation had been desperate. The danger was apparently irreversible — but God is never caught off guard. His preparation had been meticulous, His timing utterly impeccable. Read the whole book of Esther through for yourself if you want to be thrilled by the behind-the-scenes arranging of a God who never stops caring for His people.

Is your situation desperate? Does the problem seem irreversible to you? I want you to know, that though your loved-ones may seem to be in the enemy's control, God has every event monitored. He has every detail logged in His divine schedule for their lives.

Just as Esther was "come into the kingdom for such a time as this," you too are caught up in the purposes of God. You are the secret weapon in your family that God will use to turn the impossible into a glorious living reality before your eyes.

God is not limited by the forces which limit us. Nature cannot limit Him. The decrees of a king cannot limit Him. He is the only one who really can make your dreams come true.

The stories we have discussed are all found in God's infallible Word, and the wonderful news is that He "is the same yesterday, today and forever" (Hebrews 13:8). He never changes. He is always the same and He wants your household to be saved.

IT'S TIME for your family. Your "anointed moment" is on it's way. Watch for it. Believe for it — IT'S TIME.

Chapter Twelve

It's Time

In Psalm 78, the writer recounts some events from the journey of the children of Israel through the wilderness. We learn that despite the many blessings and the miraculous provision which the children of Israel experienced, they were still riddled with unbelief — so much so that they asked the question: "Can God furnish a table in the wilderness?" (Psalm 78:19).

I want you to know, that even though it may seem to you, in your situation, that you are going through a wilderness experience, God CAN spread the table of His provision for you!

The children of Israel were blinded by their unbelief. They had seen miracle after miracle, yet still they persisted to doubt God. They had seen fresh manna fall every day, to feed them. God sent them quail because they complained that they had no meat. They drank every day — IN THE MIDDLE OF THE DESERT — from the rock that followed them. Like the children of Israel, we today have been mightily blessed of God. What we cannot afford to do is ever to doubt that our God will come through for us in our wilderness.

Your family circumstances may seem like a wilderness situation at the moment, but God will always spread a table for those who trust in Him!

There is a wonderful story in Genesis Chapter 21 which I need to share with you:

Abraham had been blessed by the birth of Isaac, finally receiving the son God had promised him. Due to his previous impatience, he had already become father to another son, Ishmael, by his wife's maid, Hagar.

After a time, Abraham's wife, Sarah, saw Ishmael mocking the young Isaac. That was all the protective mother needed to insist that Ishmael and his mother Hagar be thrust out — INTO THE WILDERNESS. The only provisions they were given were some bread and a bottle of water. Soon these were used up, and the pathetic hopelessness of their calamity is expressed in the phrase: "And the water was spent in the bottle" (Genesis 21:15).

They were in the wilderness and the water was spent in their bottle. I think it would be hard to imagine a more difficult or dangerous situation than the one they were facing. Whatever difficulty you may be in, whatever the problem you may be facing in trying to win your loved-ones to Christ, your situation can be no more impossible than that of Hagar and Ishmael.

Dire though their circumstances were, God had made a promise to the young Ishmael, that he too would be the father of a mighty nation. As Hagar lifted up her voice and wept and prepared to die, God intervened and began to spread a table in the wilderness for them. The Bible says: "And God opened her eyes, and she saw a well of water" (Genesis 21:19).

They weren't just given another bottle of water, they were given a whole well — a practically limitless supply, to meet all of their future needs.

Do you feel you are in the wilderness? Does it seem that your resources are all dried up and that the water is spent in your bottle? That's the exact time when God begins to spread a table, and that's exactly the moment when He will show you that well of water flowing to meet your every need!

Throughout history there have been many times when it seemed that mankind was in a spiritual wilderness; when the water, it appeared, was spent in the bottle. There are so many instances in the Old Testament alone that we could not possibly go into them all in detail, but the stories of God intervening in the midst of a spiritual wilderness have thrilled Christians for centuries.

Time after time, in the book of Judges for instance, God answered the cry of His people to provide help and deliverance. Where there had been idolatry and sin, God spread a table in the wilderness and sent rescue through men and women anointed by the Holy Spirit.

Of all the times that there has been mass spiritual blindness and barrenness in this world, none could have been more desperate than a period just about two thousand years ago. The prophet had been silent for four hundred years. No one, it seemed, had a word from the Lord, but God always knows when IT'S TIME.

The people began to speak about a strange man. He dressed himself in camel's hair and lived on a diet of locusts and wild honey. There was something about his voice too: it was as the voice of one crying IN THE WILDERNESS, "Prepare ye the way of the Lord, make His paths straight" (Mark 1:3).

When there was no voice to be heard, God raised up a voice from the wilderness, to let mankind know that the Saviour of the world was soon to appear. It was time to spread a table. It was time to open forth a well of water that men would drink of and never thirst again: "But whosoever drinketh of the water that I shall give him shall never thirst; but the water that I shall give him shall be in him a well of water, springing up into everlasting life" (John 4:14).

It was time to redeem mankind. The Scripture says: "But when the fulness of time was come, God sent forth His Son . . ." (Galations 4:4). The only begotten Son of God took on human form and lived amidst the sons of men. Then, after thirty-three short years, three of which He spent healing, blessing and changing all who would receive from Him, the most awesome moment in history arrived. "My time is at hand," He said (Matthew 26:8).

They took the spotless Lamb of God, and with cruel, filthy hands, they nailed Him naked to a tree. They made Him a barbed crown of lance-like thorns and pressed it mercilessly into the flesh of His head. They tore the beard from His face and spat on Him; so great was their hatred; so awful was the wilderness of sin in which mankind had been entangled. His back was like a plowed field from the malicious whipping that they had subjected Him to.

The Scripture says in Isaiah 52:14, speaking prophetically of Christ, "His visage was so marred more than any man, and His form more than the sons of men." In other words, He was barely recognisable as a human being by the time that man had finished savaging Him. Little wonder that the sun would not shine, refusing to have any part in this display of unspeakable horror.

He hung there without complaint. The hymn tells us that "He could have called ten thousand angels to destroy this world, and to set Him free." In the final throes of His agony, He declared, "It is finished," and He gave up the ghost (John 19:30).

They took Him down, and laid Him in a borrowed tomb. Think of it! The Son of God had to be placed in a grave that belonged to someone else. For three days His disciples mourned, trying to reconcile themselves to the realization that all of their dreams lay buried in the tomb with Him. But they were unaware of what was really happening. The hour had finally arrived on the Divine Time-piece of the ages. I can imagine the call from God reverberating around the corridors of Heaven, "That's enough! The price for sin has been paid! — IT'S TIME!"

All of the demons of Hell must have gathered in that tomb to mock gleefully at their victory over the second Adam. But their glee would turn to despair, as Jesus descended into Hell itself, taking forever the keys of Death, Hell and the Grave. God said, "IT'S TIME," and Jesus rose from the dead, conquering the power of sin forever.

You cannot have a greater wilderness than all of mankind condemned under the power of sin. Yet, when it was time, God provided the ultimate answer. The effects of the wilderness of sin were forever nullified by the power of the shed blood of Christ. The water may have been spent in the bottle, but the well of salvation sprung open and we are still drinking from its endless supply. Salvation is still flowing like a river, and if you have let it flow into your heart, the barriers are about to break and your loved-ones are going find themselves swept along by the force of the tide. IT'S TIME.

History, since that momentous occasion, has continuously shown that whenever man found himself faced with a spiritual wilderness, God would spread a table.

The great reformation under Martin Luther

swept aside centuries of darkness, as the church again began to realise that "the just shall live by faith."

That reformation spread to my homeland of Scotland through a man named John Knox. "Give me Scotland or I die," he prayed. God answered his prayer and most of the population of Scotland, at that time, came to a saving knowledge of Jesus Christ. I pray with all my heart for such a revival to sweep again through Scotland, for right now it really is in a deep spiritual wilderness. Nevertheless, I do believe that just as it's time for your loved-ones, it's also time for a mighty outpouring in Scotland. One day you'll hear, on your daily news broadcast: "We don't know what's happening in Scotland, except that there has been an amazing spiritual awakening, and the nation is turning to God once again." Pray with me about that, won't you — IT'S TIME for Scotland.

In England, two brothers named John and Charles Wesley were used to spread a table in the wilderness. The spiritual revival they helped to begin averted the bloody slaughter of the French revolution from spreading across the channel to England.

The truth of water baptism by immersion was another table in the wilderness. In the United States, the pentecostal outpouring at Azusa Street was another. God has always been on time. He is never late. Whenever the wilderness threatened to choke the spiritual life in mankind, God always spread a table.

Where you are may well feel like a wilderness. Perhaps you feel that sin is prevailing on every corner, be it alcoholism, drugs, prostitution or whatever. You may feel like a tiny voice crying in such a vast wilderness. Whether you live in North America or Great Britain or anywhere in this world, you know the extent of the spiritual wilderness around you.

The Word of God has something to say about these particular times: "In the last days, saith God, I will pour out my Spirit upon all flesh" (Acts 2:17). We are about to see the climax of the ages, as this dispensation of time draws to a close. But before that happens, all of Heaven is going to be let loose. "The time is at hand" the Bible says (Revelation 22:10).

If you have unsaved loved-ones, they are flesh too, and therefore subject to this last day outpouring of God's precious Holy Spirit. IT'S TIME for North America. IT'S TIME for Scotland. IT'S TIME for the United Kingdom. IT'S TIME for THE WORLD! IT'S TIME for God to roll back the wilderness in your family, and spread the table of full Household Salvation. That wayward son or daughter is in your field. God won't let you lose him or her to the devil. That wife, that husband, those loved-ones you have prayed for for so long are about to discover that IT'S TIME for them too. IT'S TIME for Household Salvation. No matter how entangled your loved-ones may be in sin's wilderness, God has said that "thou shalt be saved and thy house." God will bring them in. He is about to astound you by the marvellous, mighty way in which He will cause salvation to come to your household.

God has laid the message of Household Salvation on my heart in a way that has already changed my entire life. Everywhere I minister, this message is going forth, and never, I repeat never, have I seen results such as I have been seeing. Even unsaved people are contacting me in an effort to prevent their families from being lost for eternity. How happy it makes me when I can share that salvation is for them also, and that they can be the first in their family to bruise Satan's head under their feet.

If you have never been concerned about your family's salvation, now is the time to be concerned. If you have been concerned, but have been getting discouraged, now is the time to take heart, for there is a well of water about to spring up in the wilderness for you. Believe His Word — claim the unclaimed promise. IT'S TIME for Household Salvation.

Conclusion

The truth of Household Salvation has, as I have shared with you, completely changed my life and ministry. It has become my burning desire to challenge as many as possible to begin to believe God for their families.

I know the difference it makes to be part of an entire family who love Jesus and who want to let their lives be used to glorify Him. I hope that as I have shared with you how God moved amongst the Camerons, you have seen the wonderful possibilities in your life. Today, my father is still preaching and overseeing the Bible School and Outreach Headquarters in Scotland, seeing his vision fulfilled in lives changed and separated for the work of the Gospel. My mother works right alongside him, and the work could not continue without her efforts. My sister Wendy is the school administrator, and my younger sister Louise works at her side in the office to keep things running smoothly. My brother Neil is in charge of the school teaching faculty and is assistant pastor of New Hope Church. His wife Phyllis is also full-time on staff. Louise's husband, John, teaches and is in charge of a Bible correspondence course and also runs the school printing department.

My other brother-in-law, James, who is Wendy's husband, is a master-builder, and he has been the main contractor for all of the building projects at the school. He is also a leading elder in a thriving local assembly.

Each one is deeply involved in the ministry and even their children can be found doing things like operating the church overhead projector, helping in the Sunday school, and a variety of things suitable for their ages. All of them love church, and no days are more exciting than church days!

My sister Wendy's youngest daughter, also called Wendy, is six years old. Every day after school, she comes into her mum's office to "work". She doesn't know exactly what her mother does, except that she does it in an office. Recently she was overheard to say, "When I grow up, I'm going to be an officer, just like my mother." Her confusion may sound a little amusing, but the whole point of what I have been saying to you is expressed in little Wendy's words. "Out of the abundance of the heart, the mouth speaketh."

If the Christianity you preach is the Christianity you live, nothing will influence your family more. If Christ is all-important to you, then the enthusiasm of your unreserved love for Him will captivate your loved-ones as it has captivated you. I'm believing with you for your household to be saved, but I cannot reinforce enough how important it is that you are real with God and real with your family. Be "naturally spiritual" and "spiritually natural". Don't put on a front. Don't put on your "religious voice" every time your family comes into the room. Just be yourself, in love with Jesus, and you'll do more than you could ever do by constantly "preaching" at your family.

I am convinced that God is about to sweep through the church with a tremendous outpouring of Household Salvation. It won't be just individuals coming to Christ, but whole families will be ushered into the Kingdom.

IT'S TIME for this outpouring to begin, and you need to be a part of it. Be instant in prayer; read and re-read the Scriptures telling of God's wonderful promise to you. Don't ever give up expecting God to move in your family!

IT'S TIME for your house to come to Christ. IT'S TIME FOR HOUSEHOLD SALVATION! IT'S TIME. IT'S TIME. IT'S TIME!

Available Now from Philip Cameron Ministries:
FREE – Special full color edition of the Household Salvation Prayer News – Including details of a unique prayer plan enabling you to link with Covenant Prayer Partners around the world praying every day for Household Salvation.

Also:
Further copies of the book "IT'S TIME – FOR HOUSEHOLD SALVATION" – $5.00 per copy.

Plus: An exciting teaching series on 6 one-hour audio-cassettes – THE HOUSEHOLD SALVATION SERIES – These tapes capture the thrill of 5 days of powerful ministry at PTL's Heritage USA – $25.00 per set.

Price	Item	Qty	Amount
FREE	HOUSEHOLD SALVATION PRAYER NEWS	1	FREE
$ 5.00	IT'S TIME – FOR HOUSEHOLD SALVALTION	___	$___
$25.00	THE HOUSEHOLD SALVALTION SERIES	___	$___
(All prices US currency)		TOTAL	$___

When ordering tapes or books, please add $1.00 per order for shipping and handling.

Name: _____

Address: _____

City: _____ State: _____ Zip: _____

Send to: Philip Cameron,

Box 4657,

Montgomery, Al. 36101.

Please send the names of your unsaved loved-ones to Philip Cameron and he will hold them up in prayer with you.

Name

_____

_____

_____

_____

_____

_____

_____

_____

_____

_____

_____

_____

_____

Name

_____

_____

_____

_____

_____

_____

_____

_____

_____

_____

_____

_____

_____

_____

_____

_____

_____

_____

Name

Name

Name